FATHER SOLANUS

THE STORY OF SOLANUS CASEY, O.F.M. CAP.

Catherine M. Odell

Our Sunday Visitor Publishing Division
Our Sunday Visitor, Inc.
Huntington, Indiana 46750

Other OSV books by the author:

The First Human Right: A Pro-Life Primer
(with William Odell)

•

Those Who Saw Her: The Apparitions of Mary

ISBN: 0-87973-486-8
LCCCN: 87-62387

Cover design by James E. McIlrath
Painting of Father Solanus by Nancy Dendy Geerts

PRINTED IN THE UNITED STATES OF AMERICA

486

To the wonderful Capuchins I have grown to know and love, and to my husband, Bill, who lovingly helps me to see the great joys of living in hope.

Contents

PREFACE

After eighty-six years of life, including sixty years as a religious, Father Solanus Casey, O.F.M. Cap., had very little which could be called "personal effects." Several days after his death in Detroit, Michigan, on July 31, 1957, his Capuchin brothers went to his small room at St. Bonaventure's Friary to collect his things.

There was a black brimmed winter hat, a brown skull cap, some family photos, letters, a trunk, some books, a pair of wire-rimmed glasses, a pair of shoes, a winter overcoat, a second pair of sandals, some underclothes and nightshirts, a breviary, a violin with bow, several pictures of the Blessed Virgin, a rosary, two worn habits, and the red stole he'd worn each Wednesday at the 3:00 P.M. healing service. It was a poor man's holdings.

A much larger legacy of the man did exist. It was the kind that couldn't be counted or evaluated in terms of dollars and cents.

"Some years ago I was in utter despair and just wanted to die," confessed a tearful woman at the Capuchin's wake. "I spoke to him and began to live again."

"Fifteen years ago, my son was dying of polio," a parent reported. "Father Solanus blessed him and today he is in the best of health."

There were hundreds — even thousands — of such stories. They all had a common theme. Father Solanus had prayed, and things were never the same again. Many times, things changed for the better. People with cancer, paralysis, blindness, emotional illness, and tumors were among those who claimed healings through this priest. Others realized that Solanus was preparing them to accept death, the loss of a loved one, or continued suffering.

5

Father Solanus was ordained a priest in 1904, but he was denied the faculties to hear confessions or to give doctrinal sermons. For want of a better way to employ him, this priest was given the job of friary porter, or doorkeeper. He answered the door and took messages. Gradually, however, friary visitors found something spiritually magnetic about the kind bearded priest. They began to tell him of their problems and their hopes. He reminded them of the goodness of God. He promised to pray for their needs, and did so, even into the loneliest hours of the night.

Into this humble vessel, this doorkeeper, great spiritual gifts began to be poured. When Father Solanus prayed for others, his prayers were answered with unexplainable frequency. He was able to foresee future events and often shared his visions with others. In today's light, it seems evident that Father Solanus had been given the gifts of miracles, prophecy, healing, discernment, and other gifts of the Spirit described by St. Paul in 1 Corinthians 12. Father Solanus also had mighty gifts of faith, hope, and love that overflowed into all that he said and did.

His was a life that changed others, often after no more than a momentary meeting. His closeness to the Lord was so apparent that people of all ages, creeds, economic backgrounds, and cultures were drawn to him. An investigation of his cause for beatification and canonization is currently under way. As a result, he may one day be named as the first native-born American male canonized as a saint. Father Solanus himself might have blushed at the prospect. Throughout his life, he constantly asked his friends to pray for his own conversion and salvation.

Father Solanus Casey is an awesome and yet accessible model for our modern times. His virtues and story "translate" especially well for today's American Christians. The son of Irish immigrants, he was a Midwesterner from a big family who loved baseball, hot dogs with onions, and could shoot a fair game of pool. He was also a pilgrim in our own century of telephones, TVs, the Cold War, and consumerism. The special blessing of Father Solanus to American Catholics and all Christians is that he showed others that a life-giving faith and love of God could be so simple yet so powerful.

One day, during the Detroit days of Father Solanus, a small boy with a cast on his arm sat in the front waiting room of St. Bonaventure's Friary. After dozens of others moved ahead to ask the bearded Capuchin for a blessing, the boy finally moved to the porter's desk with his mother. He had heard of the wonderful healings accomplished through this priest's prayers. Suddenly, to the mother's surprise, the boy began to tug anxiously at the cast encasing his arm.

The friar with the warm blue eyes and smile leaned over the desk to speak to the boy. He knew what the child was thinking. "God's blessing goes right on through," Father Solanus reassured the boy. With that, he blessed the youngster's arm — cast and all — and then the mother. The boy's face lit up with understanding and peace. He smiled back at Father Solanus and took him at his word.

ACKNOWLEDGMENTS

Every story must have a beginning, a middle, and an ending. Even though Father Solanus Casey has been dead since 1957, his story does not seem to be ending. People from all over the world are hearing of him and passing along the accounts of his life. The cause of his beatification and subsequent canonization is under consideration by the Sacred Congregation for the Causes of Saints. So, Rome is also hearing his story.

This version of Solanus's story traces its beginning to the decade of life (1946-1956) which Father Solanus lived out at St. Felix Friary in Huntington, Indiana. Early in 1956, he was transferred back to Detroit where he died in 1957. When this author lived in Huntington, twenty years after his death, people were still talking of him, telling their own stories about him.

This author is grateful to the copyright holders of various works cited in the Bibliography, portions of which have served as the basis for this book. Grateful thanks is given particularly to the authors of two earlier biographies of Father Solanus. The foundations of their research also contributed greatly to this book's beginning.

In 1968, a book by James Patrick Derum, *The Porter of St. Bonaventure's*, was published by Fidelity Press in Detroit. Derum had met Father Solanus once in the early 1930s and was able to interview Monsignor Edward Casey, the only surviving brother of Father Solanus, in 1961. (Monsignor Edward died the following year.)

In 1985, *Thank God Ahead of Time: The Life and Spirituality of Solanus Casey* was published by Franciscan Herald Press of Chicago. The author was Father Michael Crosby, O.F.M. Cap., who told his richly documented "story" of Solanus from the perspective of a fellow Capuchin.

Great thanks are also due to Brother Leo Wollenweber, O.F.M. Cap., vice-postulator of the cause of beatification and canonization for Father Solanus. Brother Leo's personal memories of Father Solanus and his cooperation in opening the archives of Solanus material to this author were invaluable contributions. Direct quotations from the writings of Father Solanus (notably in the section headed "Words and Wisdom of Father Solanus" in the latter part of this work) have been left intact — grammatical inconsistencies and all — to maintain the flavor and spirit of the Capuchin's innermost thoughts.

Last but not least, it should be pointed out that all photographs appearing in this book have been made available through the courtesy of the *Detroit News*, the Father Solanus Guild in Detroit, *The Michigan Catholic*, and various individuals, whose kindness in loaning these photographs helped make this work possible.

CHAPTER ONE

The Caseys Homestead in America (1865-1882)

It was the twenty-fifth of November, 1870 — exactly one month before Christmas. A newborn's cry could again be heard inside the Caseys' three-room log house near Oak Grove, Wisconsin, just south of Prescott. The snow-topped cabin was perched upon a bluff high above the mighty Mississippi River, which in this vicinity formed a boundary between Wisconsin and Minnesota. Here, the Mississippi was "modest" and not quite so "mighty."

In this western Wisconsin county, farmland had still been available when Bernard and Ellen Casey arrived from Pennsylvania in 1865. Ellen's two brothers had raved about the good land they were already farming along the river in Prescott, Wisconsin. Bernard, or "Barney" (as his friends and acquaintances called him), had laid claim to eighty acres next to theirs. The farm was about twenty-five miles from St. Paul, across the river and about two hundred miles from the place where the Mississippi River has its origins. Like everything else, the river had to have its own beginning.

Even the snug Irish Catholic family so at home inside the cabin had origins far from Wisconsin and Minnesota. Barney and Ellen had finally settled far from the Irish counties where they had both been born. They were, as historians later dubbed them, "Potato Irish," immigrants from Ireland who'd come to America during and after the years of Ireland's Great Potato Famine of the 1840s. Without industrial development in Ireland, there was no other alternative.

Bernard and his Ellen did not really know the size of this migration from their native Ireland. They knew only that they'd had plenty of Irish company on the crossing boats. Historians confirmed their impressions by noting later that four million Irish had sailed across the Atlantic Ocean to America from 1845 to 1900.[1] "Poor Ireland's done," "the country's gone forever," Irish immigrants told one another in this country.[2]

While the Caseys were still thinking of a name for the newborn boy on this cold day in 1870, his mother, Ellen Elizabeth Murphy Casey, was resting. She herself had also been born on a wintry day — January 9, 1844.

Ellen had been born in Camlough in County Armagh in what is now Northern Ireland. The Irish cherished County Armagh for its connection with St. Patrick. In the fifth century, according to tradition, the great St. Patrick had put up a church there in Armagh. Armagh, therefore, was soaked in the traditions of the Church. Ellen had carried that well-rooted love of faith to America as a very young child.

Ellen's father died in County Armagh during the famine that had scourged Ireland from 1846 to 1849. The famine occurred because a blight ruined the potato crop for several years in a row. On the table and as a crop, the potato was the staple for this small island nation. One-fourth of the arable land of Ireland had been planted in potatoes.[3]

After their father's death, little Ellen Murphy, an older sister, Mary Ann, and their three brothers, Patrick, Owen, and Maurice, along with their mother, Brigid Shields Murphy, crossed the Atlantic to America. They arrived in Boston around 1852. Brigid and her family came first to the Boston area, where she had relatives on the Shields side. But soon after arriving, Brigid traveled with her five children to Portland, Maine. There, she and her two older sons went to work in the textile mills. There were few alternatives. Like most of the Irish who came, there was almost no money left once passage was paid for. Nonetheless, hard, grinding twelve-hour days, six-day weeks provided little more than a subsistence income. Ellen and Mary Ann boarded with a Portland housewife in exchange for light housekeeping chores. The baby, three-year-old Maurice, was cared for by a family friend.

After almost ten years of scrimping and hard labor, Brigid had money enough to move west to the region around St. Paul, Minnesota. Patrick and Owen, young men by then, had already found work there. Brigid's older daughter, Mary Ann, had married and moved there, too. Ellen, however, had stayed behind to live and work in Biddeford, Maine. Now almost grown up, she was a petite, lovely young woman with straight facial features and deep-set blue eyes.

At a Fourth of July picnic, in 1860, sixteen-year-old Ellen Murphy met Bernard James Casey, the brother of her friend Ellen Casey. A tall, handsome dark-haired young man, Bernard told Ellen that he'd come from County Monoghan three years earlier. She said she'd been born in Armagh. They both may have laughed at this exchange of information. County Monoghan and Armagh were neighboring counties in the north of Ireland and yet the two of them had traveled all the way to America before they met. (Although they are neighboring counties, County Monoghan remained part of the Republic of Ireland while County Armagh became part of Northern Ireland when that island nation was split into two countries in 1920.)

Young Casey had just turned twenty several weeks before meeting Ellen. He had been born June 10, 1840, at Castleblayney in County Monoghan. County Monoghan, an area known as one of the richest fishing spots in Ireland, bragged of more than one hundred eighty lakes. But young Bernard had decided to leave the lovely lakes behind. In 1857, along with his sister, Ellen, the seventeen-year-old left Ireland behind for America. In the Boston area, their brother Terrence was already becoming established. Once he'd settled in, Bernard learned the shoemaking trade and soon went into business with Terrence.[4]

Apparently, Bernard and Ellen felt drawn to each other from that Fourth of July meeting. In the months that followed, they saw each other often. Before long, Barney had proposed marriage, and Ellen wrote to her mother in Hastings, Minnesota, about her thoughts of marriage.

Ellen's mother may have been hundreds of miles away, but her authority was persuasive at any distance. She did not want her daughter married at so young an age. She sent for Ellen and Ellen traveled to Minnesota. The Casey-Murphy romance then had to be conducted via letters.

As the months went by, it was clear to Brigid that the relationship would survive the difficulties of courtship by letter — all the way from Hastings, Minnesota, to Boston. Brigid finally gave her approval to the marriage. On October 6, 1863, Ellen and Barney were married in a small church in Salem, a Boston suburb. The bridegroom was twenty-three, his bride was nineteen.

For a while, the young couple lived in Boston. The Civil War had begun two years before, and wartime demand for shoes by the Union army kept the Casey brothers busy making shoes. By the end of the war in April, 1865, however, the demand fell drastically. The Northern armies disbanded and no longer ordered shoes by the hundreds.

Bernard and Ellen Casey began to move westward in stages. They were looking for a livelihood. They lived in Germantown, Pennsylvania, for a few months and then went to New Castle. There, Bernard and Terrence opened a shoe store, but the brothers quickly saw that making and selling shoes would no longer provide them with a good living. They split up. Terrence decided to move back east to attend law school.[5]

For the young Caseys, however, the move to farming and

to the Midwest seemed to be their only course. In 1862, Congress had passed the Homestead Act, which granted one hundred sixty acres to anyone wishing to settle on and cultivate public lands for at least five years. Variations on this "homesteading" concept had been adapted in many areas. The couple already had two children to support. Little Ellen had been born July 8, 1864, and James had been born August 14, 1865.

Sometime in the autumn of 1865, Barney and Ellen Casey moved into the area near Prescott, Wisconsin. A small log cabin was soon put up as was a shelter for a pair of oxen and a cow. Barney watched with amazement as his brothers-in-law showed him how to use the steel plow to break the ground.[6] The little family of four settled in, and the head of the house registered his claim. Crops were planted during the following spring.

Most Irish immigrants who'd come to America were settling in urban areas in the East, since they lacked the capital to move west. And despite the fact that the Irish had come from rural settings, American agriculture on the frontier was very different than growing potatoes, or "murphies," on their small plots in close-knit communities in Ireland.[7] In this respect, the Caseys were unusual, but they were not alone.

Although German immigrants outnumbered the Irish in Wisconsin in census reports for 1870, the Irish constituted the second largest group of foreign-born until 1870. Then the Norwegians poured into the state, overtaking the Irish immigrants for a ranking behind the Germans.[8] On the whole, the Midwest was clearly developing a German flavor. German immigrants were settling in such numbers in the Midwest that Cincinnati, Milwaukee, and St. Louis were said to form a "German Triangle."[9]

Like many Wisconsin farms, the land Barney Casey staked had been selected for its combination of wooded acreage and prairie land. The woods provided fuel and building materials while the prairie was relatively easy to clear for planting. Pierce County apparently still had plenty of room to offer to newcomers. An 1860 county census, taken only five years before the Caseys arrived, showed that only eighty-two families, including seven Irish families, were then settled there.[10] Though Irish neighbors were few in number, Bernard Casey felt more at home in farming than he'd been in business in the city. He meant to make it work for himself and for his growing family.

The seasons of planting and harvest passed by quickly. Wisconsin had become a central part of the new "wheat boom," and the Caseys planted their share of it. New strains of wheat had been developed which produced bigger yields. By the 1860s, Milwaukee was rivaling Chicago as the greatest wheat-shipping port in the world.[11]

The family was flourishing, too. Mary Ann was born to the Caseys on September 19, 1866. Maurice was born November 7, 1867, and John was born February 10, 1869. Tiny John was just old enough to toddle around the bed where this new baby, born in November of 1870, was lying in Ellen's arms.

There were six little Caseys on the Prescott place now. With another healthy child born to them and with a good harvest gathered in that year, Ellen and Barney Casey had plenty to be thankful for on this November twenty-fifth. They may have heard of the Thanksgiving holiday that the late President Abraham Lincoln had established in 1863 in the midst of the Civil War.

The baby exercising his lungs was the fourth boy born to the Caseys. He had the Casey dark hair and blue eyes. Ellen and Barney believed that all their children were special gifts from the God they vigorously believed in. And yet, Bernard Casey, talking it over with his wife, must have seen this new child in a slightly different light. After three sons, he decided to give this son his own first name.

The sixth child was therefore called Bernard Francis Casey. On December 18, 1870, with Christmas in the air, the baby was baptized at St. Joseph's Church in Prescott, a few miles from the homestead.[12] At home, the baby was called "Barney," his father's nickname.

Little Barney learned to walk in the increasingly cramped

15

cabin. He grew used to the noise of the rolling Mississippi below the bluffs. The sound of the water was one of his earliest memories along with the distant image of his mother hanging laundry on the lines near the house. His mother would shout news across the river to Mrs. Cotter, their neighbor.[13]

By the age of two, little Barney may have been paying some attention to family prayer as well. It was a nightly custom in this cabin near Prescott. Slowly, he was learning to recognize certain prayers, including the prayers of the Rosary. Though he would not have understood the meaning of such a prayer, little Barney even heard the older Caseys ask "for a happy death and a favorable judgment."[14]

During these evening prayers, the Casey toddlers undoubtedly moved around the table from father's to mother's lap. Some impression became fixed in the consciousness of the children. Prayer was talking. Adults talked a lot. Adults talked to one another and to children. Prayer was simply talking to an unseen God.

For children living on the land in the last quarter of the nineteenth century there was no reason to question the reality of unseen powers. Summer storms, winter whiteouts, blazing prairie fires, abundant harvests, the flowing Mississippi River nearby — all these things were the result of great powers which could not be comprehended, though the work of those powers could be seen. And in the Casey setting, the God spoken to was immediately recognized as a God who loved his children just as Bernard and Ellen loved their children.

There were many intentions to be prayed for in this daily routine of prayer. Like other nineteenth-century pioneers, the Caseys were aware of their need for "daily bread." Practically, it was fashioned from the wheat and other crops they raised and harvested. But they understood that there was a merciful Father, a Creator who gave growth to the wheat in the first place.

Therefore, in the Casey cabin, there was prayer for rain, prayer to be spared from ravaging insects, blights, or molds, and prayer for dry days to harvest when the crops were ready.

16

There were also prayers raised to avoid prairie fires and prayers offered for the protection of livestock — chickens, cows, the team of oxen, horses, and pigs. The Caseys prayed and never really got finished with praying. The needs were many.

Living was still pretty rough in western Wisconsin in those days. Cabins, like the one the Caseys were living in, were literally rough. Logs were unhewed, chinked in between with mud. The cabins were roofed with shakes and floored with rough planks. Furniture was also scanty and crude.[15]

By 1873, Bernard Casey, Sr., had begun to set his heart on a larger place. The fine harvests of recent years had given him the chance to save some money. But the main reason was that his family was still growing. Since the birth of little Barney in 1870, Patrick had been born March 22, 1872, and a new baby was due in the spring of 1874. The head of the family had discovered a more spacious place for sale not far from his Prescott farm. Before the end of 1873, he bought it and moved his clan and all their belongings to a new homestead. It was a little farther to the east.

When the family moved to the new property in Trimbelle township, the world for three-year-old Barney, Jr., naturally expanded. The new Trimbelle homestead was close to a river with the same name which flowed into the Mississippi just north of Redwing, Minnesota. This farm had a bigger house and was closer to a Catholic church and school.

Little Barney was to remember this second place more clearly than the property near Prescott. The house near Trimbelle, Wisconsin, he estimated later, was about twelve by thirty feet with a partial loft for sleeping. The Casey boys had the run of the loft. Their sisters, far fewer in number, bedded down on one side of a divider on the ground floor. The parents slept on the other side of the divider. Otherwise, the cabin was entirely open, with no other rooms.[16]

Much of the country surrounding the Caseys must have seemed quite rugged. "Wild beasts and rattlesnakes seem to have been the most common cause of such anxiety," recalled

17

Bernard Casey, Jr., later.[17] He was thinking of the worries his parents had about the safety of their children in this Wisconsin wilderness. Once, some of the boys even came face-to-face with a bear that chased them.

Some of the dangers of this area, however, had nothing to do with wild animals.

On one summer Sunday during a dry spell in these homesteading mid-1870s, a prairie fire licked its way across the grasslands in the direction of the Casey homestead. Black smoke billowed toward the house and was blown ahead by the stiff winds. Prairie fires terrorized homesteaders. Houses, barns, and crops were sometimes consumed in an hour's time.

Barney, Sr., and about half of his children were away at church on this particular Sunday. Since the Casey wagon would carry only about half of his large family to Mass six miles away, the other half remained home and prayed. Thomas had been born March 11, 1874, Martha on May 5, 1875, Augustine on June 14, 1876, and Leo on March 10, 1878. On the following Sunday, the children who had remained home the previous Sunday went with their mother while the others stayed home with their father.

As soon as she saw the fire, Ellen gathered up her children, took them out of the house, and huddled with them near a tree in one of the fields. For a while, it looked as though the house would be lost. She told young Ellen, her oldest child, to quickly hoe a firebreak in front of the house and pour holy water along it as a prayer. Though the barn was burned to the ground, the fire stopped short of the house.

Little Barney hid his face in his mother's skirts to avoid the stifling smell of the smoke. Finally, he heard her nervous breathing change. "Thank God," she murmured. One of the neighbors had run over to let the hog out of the pen adjacent to the barn. The frantic animal escaped just before the barn exploded into flames. When little Barney's father and the other children came home at about noon, it was all over. The barn was destroyed, but nothing else, including field crops, had been lost.[18]

Despite the natural risks of life on the frontier, there were many compensations as well. There was a wild beauty that all the Casey children remembered long into adulthood when most lived in metropolitan areas.

"How rich in its variety and abundance of wild flowers and fruits and nuts and berries," wrote Barney, Jr., years later when he was a priest. "There was a pasture field for cattle as well as deer and other animals." In apparent curiosity, deer would often stop in twos and threes to watch the strange things being done by the two-legged Caseys going about their farming chores.[19]

In 1878, a different kind of disaster hit the Caseys. The loss was much more devastating than any loss by prairie fire could have been.

Twelve-year-old Mary Ann, the second daughter, was struck with "black diphtheria." A highly contagious disease seen often in this era, diphtheria epidemics were common in the U.S. and western Europe. The upper respiratory system was typically affected with a thick membrane forming up and down the air passages. Victims, usually children, ran high fevers, had sore throats, and sometimes died when the deadly membrane literally closed air passages.

There was little that Bernard and Ellen could do for their Mary Ann. She died after struggling for several days for breath. But the tragedy was not over. Within three days of Mary Ann's death, three-year-old Martha also died in the same way. Two children dead in less than a week! The Caseys were grief-stricken but had little time to mourn their daughters.

Several of the boys, including eight-year-old Barney, also came down with the disease. Trying to isolate their sick children, the parents hovered over their sons who were struggling to catch their breath. The prayers of the parents were answered. All of the boys recovered but not without some side effects. Barney was left with injured vocal cords where the membranes had formed and infected his throat. From then on, his voice was weakened, somewhat high-pitched, and wispy, even into manhood.[20]

The loss of Mary Ann and Martha was always sharp for the Caseys, even though their family still numbered nine children after the death of the girls. The Caseys believed very firmly that Mary Ann and little Martha were with God. Life continued. Although the two Casey girls died from disease, over twenty percent of frontier children, in the 1880s, died before they reached five years of age for other reasons. Death was usually due to primitive housing conditions and poor sanitation.[21] Bernard Casey, Sr., was doing his best to house and feed his children well. Unlike many farmers, he fed his milk cows over winter and always had a large garden to provide fresh fruits and vegetables.

By the early 1880s, the Casey family circle expanded with more children, apparently crowding the little house to its limits. After the death of the little girls in 1878, Edward had been born in July of 1879 and Owen had been born in January of 1881. By the summer of 1882, eleven-year-old Barney was in the older half of a clan of eleven Casey children. In order, they were eighteen-year-old Ellen, seventeen-year-old Jim, fourteen-year-old Maurice (who was entering the diocesan seminary at Milwaukee), thirteen-year-old John, Barney, ten-year-old Pat, eight-year-old Tom, six-year-old Gus, four-year-old Leo, three-year-old Ed, and one-year-old Owen. With such a houseful of children, life was not easy on a day-to-day basis. But it seemed to be rich.

There was an order to the Casey life. In part, it was set by the seasons and the need to gain a living from the land. Inside the house, however, the parents, Ellen and Bernard, Sr., saw to it that another order, the spiritual order, was clearly visible to their children. By the early 1880s, the Irish-born head of the Casey clan began to look for a larger frontier on which to settle his growing American enterprise — his family and his farm.

CHAPTER TWO

Growing Up Well Rooted (1882-1891)

In the summer of 1882, Bernard Casey, Sr., the father and head of this American Casey clan, was forty-two years old. He was well built, of average height, and was still a very sturdy man. A wiry black beard circled this patriarch's chin, trimmed according to the custom of the day. Well respected among his neighbors, Casey had farmed the Trimbelle place for just short of nine years. During those years, the Casey crops had been bountiful. The family, too, had grown to thirteen with eleven living children, and Ellen was expecting another baby in September.

Sometime during 1882, Barney, Sr., had heard of a 345-acre spread for sale just to the north of Pierce County. The property was in St. Croix County. Bernard Casey had ridden up to look at it. The place had a six-room clapboard house, two barns, a large icehouse, a root house, and a lake on the property.[1] Looking it over was like entering a dream.

The Willow River, which flowed close by the good-sized farm, intrigued the Irish homesteader. Equally intriguing to Barney Casey was the fact that a railroad line ran through the property and made a stop just two miles away. Easy transportation, by rail or by river, would be assured for his crops. He went home to think about it. But in a short while, the deal was made. The Caseys were to move again.

Like the rest of the family, Barney, Jr., was thrilled with the new spread. Though he knew he would miss the place where he had spent most of his childhood, the lake, larger fields, and sheer size of the new property better fitted the scope of his twelve-year-old tastes for adventure and outdoor fun.

On September 23, 1882, Barney's baby sister, Margaret, was born. As always, there was plenty of rejoicing over the new baby. But Margaret's birth was even more special. Until Margaret came, there had been only one girl among the eleven living Casey children, Mary Ann and Martha having both died in 1878. She was the oldest child, eighteen-year-old Ellen.

After the baby was born and the harvesting was completed came the awesome job of moving. It had to be done with one eye to the calendar and the other on the sky. The move had to be made before a sudden snowfall could block the roads and make the move treacherous.

All the household supplies along with the farm equipment had to be transported. There were also chickens, cattle, horses, pigs, and assorted pets to transport. But finally the Caseys were tucked in at their new home before the Wisconsin winter could catch them on the open road. Bernard Casey, Sr., must have smiled broadly at the blessings from heaven. He had been given such a fine farm and a healthy, happy family, including a second daughter.

Except for tending to the livestock, winters meant some time off for Midwestern farmers like Barney Casey, Sr. Therefore, Casey resolved to find a way to turn the slack season to good purpose. He became a distributor of religious books and also sold subscriptions to the *Irish Standard* and the *Extension Magazine*. He traveled to St. Paul by train and returned with the books, heaving them off into the snowbank as the train passed near the Casey homestead. Knowing about what time the train passed through, several of the older Casey boys would pick up the canvas sack heavy with books and put it on the wagon. Bernard Casey, Sr., would walk back home from the Burkhardt stop two miles away.[2]

The Caseys enjoyed literature and music. In addition to the religious books that they were allowed to read if they did not soil them, they enjoyed other literature. The works of James Fenimore Cooper, especially *The Deerslayer*, were family favorites. After dinner, Barney, Sr., would often push his chair back from the table after prayer was concluded, hoist the youngest child up on his lap, and read aloud.

Stories about Abraham Lincoln, the verses of Irish poet Thomas Moore, and the poems of American poet Henry Wadsworth Longfellow were fondly remembered by the younger Caseys years later. In particular, the Casey children loved one long poem by the American poet John Greenleaf Whittier called "Snow-Bound."[3] "And ere the early bedtime came / The white drift piled the window-frame, / And through the glass the clothes-line posts / Looked in like tall and sheeted ghosts," Greenleaf wrote. It was a lovely vision the Caseys had seen winter after winter.

Ellen and Bernard Casey also made sure that their American-born children were well acquainted with their Irish heritage. They passed on the stories and legends of their homeland. With a fiddle bought somewhere along the way, the head of the house would also play and lead his household in singing Irish ballads. If he lacked anything in musical polish, his children saw that their father compensated for it with enthusiasm.

If the railroad was helping to expand literary horizons for the Caseys of St. Croix County, the railroad was also becoming responsible for some very practical benefits. Before the advent of the railroads and the 1880s, all time throughout the country was local time. A clock in Milwaukee might be reading 11:05 at the same moment that a Chicago timepiece was striking 11:00. On Sunday, November 18, 1883, however, railroads throughout the U.S. adopted "Standard Time" to allow the trains to run "on time." People commonly went to railroad stations after that to get the exact time when the signal came over the telegraph.[4]

Life on the Casey farm was running on its own schedule, and the patterns of religious practice and faith were unchanging. The weekly Sunday trip to Mass was now a bit farther than it had been on the Trimbelle property. St. Patrick's Church at Hudson, Wisconsin, was nine miles from the Casey home. Each Sunday, at least some members of the Casey family were represented, starting out for church a full two hours before the scheduled Mass.[5] And as the family settled into its new home during the winter of 1882-1883, the tradition of evening prayer continued. As soon as dinner was over, Bernard, Sr., called for quiet and began the prayers, including the Rosary.

At twelve, young Barney was starting to grow much faster. The bout with diphtheria at seven had left his voice weakened and wispy, and he did not seem as strong as some of his brothers. Nonetheless, he was strong enough and loved the outdoor life. With blue eyes and dark hair, he looked much like the other Casey boys, but there was something a bit more gentle about his face and behavior.

Though Barney played baseball aggressively, especially as a catcher, he refused to take part in the boxing matches the other Casey boys set up near the barn.[6] His coolness to the sport mystified his brothers. It was, after all, the era of the great prizefighter John L. Sullivan.

In 1882, Sullivan defeated Paddy Ryan to win the heavyweight boxing crown, and J.L. was to hang on to the title for ten years! But Barney would not touch the gloves that his brothers had pooled their money to buy. He gave no reasons for his distaste, and after a while his brothers did not pressure him.

In the spring of 1883, the Caseys saw Maurice leave home to enter St. Francis Seminary in Milwaukee. At the same time, Barney eagerly traveled into Hudson to spend two weeks in preparation for his First Holy Communion. Twelve was the customary age for First Communicants in this era. Father Thomas A. Kelley, the pastor of St. Patrick's at Hudson, wanted to make sure that his communicants were well drilled in the faith before they received the sacrament. Barney also "took the Pledge," agreeing to abstain from alcohol until he was twenty-one years of age.[7]

It was the custom then in Irish communities to ask young boys to make that promise before receiving First Communion. In 1840, the Fourth Provincial Council of Baltimore had recommended the establishment of "temperance" societies in all parishes to curb alcohol use. The first statewide Wisconsin meeting of the Catholic Total Abstinence Society had been held in 1871.

But the enthusiasm to spread the "Pledge" was primarily an Irish interest. German Catholics didn't participate, and one German priest offered a somewhat slanted explanation for their attitude. The "Pledge" movement was a good idea for the English and Irish, he said, because "as everybody knows, they drink solely to get drunk" while Germans knew how to drink with moderation.[8]

During the summer and autumn following his First Communion, Barney began to say his own Rosary each night in addition to the family's recitation. He would kneel by the side of his bed and pray it quietly. At the time of his First Communion, there had been a powerful experience of the Blessed Virgin Mary.

One night, Barney had a dream about the Rosary. It came after an exhausting day. Because he ached with muscle strain and fatigue, Barney had headed toward bed, thinking that he might skip his Rosary just for that night. His brothers were already in bed. The Casey house was growing quiet. The teenager wanted only to drop into bed and go to sleep. But instead, he dropped to his knees. He knelt upright, not leaning on the bed. He had seen his mother and sister Ellen pray that way as long as he could remember.

Wishing to keep the commitment to this prayer, Barney had determined to recite at least one decade of the Rosary. To his surprise, the weariness left him and he completed the full five decades. Later that night, he dreamed that he was hanging over a huge pit with flames licking up toward him. Desperately, he looked around to see a way out. Finally, he realized that a large rosary was dangling just above his head. In the shadowy reality of dreams, he grabbed on to it and suddenly felt secure. The dream impressed the boy greatly.[9]

If Barney showed signs of deep love of prayer, he was also very clearly fond of adventure and outdoor life. He was constantly devising ingenious ways to snare prairie chickens or rabbits. It was also Barney who knew right where the wild berries were and where to get the wild hops his mother needed for yeast.[10] This Casey farm at Hudson was much larger than the Trimbelle property had been. Barney's older brothers, Jim and John, began to share the heavier farming jobs with their father. In turn, Barney "inherited" some of the chores his older brothers had always done. Some he relished.

When eighteen-year-old Jim, Barney's oldest brother, got a new rifle, Barney began to shadow him. Barney was keenly interested in hunting. Since small game and even an occasional deer helped to feed the large Casey clan, hunting was a serious business and not merely sport. More and more, Jim turned his rifle over to Barney. Often with a friend, Chris Adams, Barney went hunting regularly. He became a good shot and could typically be counted upon to bag rabbits, wild ducks, geese, or prairie chickens. With perhaps a bit less enthusiasm, he also chopped wood, weeded the garden, looked for eggs the chickens laid, and fed and watered the stock.

Barney, Jr., became aware that the usual family petitions for good crops carried a tone of greater and greater need. Clearly, his father was becoming more and more concerned about the situation. During the later months of 1882, a special petition was added to the Caseys' night prayer which asked the Lord to spare the crops from total disaster.

Until the 1880s, wheat was the principal crop for Wisconsin farmers such as Bernard Casey, Sr. Within that decade, however, the soil on many farms was becoming depleted through the continual use of fields for wheat. Plagues of chinch bugs had also begun to threaten wheat's prominence.[11] Farm prices were falling and had been falling for some time. To add to the farmers' grief, their hard times were arriving at a time when manufactured goods were becoming more expensive. American industry was booming.[12]

By the time he was fourteen, Barney was slender but strong and wiry. He had not yet completed his elementary schooling, but that was not unusual. In agricultural communities, schooling had to follow a different sort of schedule. Fields had to be planted in the spring and crops had to be harvested when the time was right. Children, especially the boys, were needed to help, and schooling had to be fitted around the needs of agriculture.

During these hard months a day came that provided Barney with enough excitement and fun to compensate for a heavier load of responsibilities.

Out in the fields with three of his younger brothers, fifteen-year-old Barney and fourteen-year-old Pat suddenly froze in their tracks. Rover, the family dog, bounded into view. He was excited and bleeding from a slash down his shoulder. Barney and Pat understood what it was all about when they heard a wildcat snarling from a tree not far from where they stood. Brave Rover had tangled with the cat and had been cut up for his efforts.

Barney knew that there was no way to keep Rover from going at it again. And having a wildcat so close to the house and to smaller children was dangerous. Without his rifle, the cat would have to be bagged some other way. "Go on up to the top of the bank and stay up there," Barney warned the other two brothers. He and Pat would handle the cat with Rover's help.

Immediately, Rover returned to snap at the cat, but the cat suddenly leaped down on him. Dog and wildcat tumbled over and over. Pat picked up a big stick with which to hit the cat which was clawing their Rover. Barney circled to within two feet of the scrapping animals and cautiously lifted a large rock. Holding it poised, he waited for Rover to move away from the cat. At just the right moment, Barney heaved the rock toward the cat. He hit the animal squarely on the head and it dropped dead where it was. Rover sniffed at the animal which was suddenly still. The little boys whooped from the top of the bank and came running down to their brave brothers, Barney and Pat.

The two older Casey boys found some vines and a tree branch and strung the dead animal from it. Thinking perhaps of Nattie Bumpo, the frontier woodsman they'd "met" in the books of James Fenimore Cooper, the bigger boys proudly carried the cat home. There was a bounty on wildcats, so Barney and Pat knew that the carcass would bring a much needed ten dollars into the family coffers. But on the way home, Barney thought of a way to get something else out of the dead cat.

A little later, a ferocious wildcat was "ready to spring" just outside the family home. Propped up just a bit, the animal looked menacing enough. Pat raced into the house and told his parents that a wildcat was crouching outside. The whole family edged just outside the door to peek. While the rest of the Caseys stood ready to rush for the door, Barney and the other boys ran from behind the trees exposing the joke. By the end of the day four Casey boys were still hooting with delight at the terror their "dangerous" wildcat had caused.[13]

With disappointing harvests in 1885 and 1886, Barney's studies were pushed back even farther. Along with older brothers and a sister, the boy had to look for extra work to help support the family. Barney Casey, Sr., was worried but thanked the Lord for his children who could now help save his family from desperate need.[14] Each evening during the bleak winter of 1885, he added a prayer to the evening family prayers, asking for some profit from the crops the Caseys had worked so hard to raise. (During this time of uncertainty, Grace, the Caseys' fifteenth child, was born on March 3, 1885. The last of the Casey children, Genevieve, would be born almost three years later to the day: March 7, 1888.)

During the following year, 1886, young Barney went to Stillwater, Minnesota, a town about twenty miles from the Casey homestead. Like his older brother Jim, Barney set out to find some work because farming income for the year had been very poor. Stillwater was a good choice, Barney's parents thought, because Father Maurice Murphy, Ellen's younger brother, was pastor of the parish there. Ellen was very close to her brother and had rowed up and down the St. Croix River raising pledges for the church he was trying to build.[15] Barney could live with his uncle.

Barney found a job at the lumber mill in Stillwater. Lumbering, a massive enterprise in the white pine forests of Wisconsin during the last half of the nineteenth century, provided seasonal work for farmers. Some say that four-hundred-year-old pines, up to ten feet in diameter, were not uncommon finds; but they were cut down in the same fashion as thousands of others.[16]

Working on the catwalks built above the water in Stillwater, young Barney became a "river driver" and guided the logs floating down the St. Croix River from lumbering camps toward the mill. When the mercury plunged and the river froze over, Barney went home. The logs would remain frozen upriver in massive logjams until the spring thaw. At home, Barney wanted to continue to work at his schooling.

With what Barney and his brothers had made and with the proceeds from the harvest, Bernard, Sr., was able to pay off debts and end the year with a surplus. By then, Maurice was also contributing toward this effort. After three years, the nineteen-year-old had left the seminary due to a condition called neurasthenia. It was a type of neurosis marked by fatigue, weakness, irritability, and localized pains. The return of Maurice from the seminary was a great disappointment to his parents. Ellen tried not to show it, but the head of the house had less success in hiding his distress.

As he was finishing up his schooling, Barney met a girl named Rebecca Tobin. Rebecca's family lived on a neighboring farm. She was soft-spoken and had dark hair and dark eyes. Barney may have known her for some time, but a new feeling developed between them following a debate he participated in near his sixteenth birthday, in November of 1886.

Public debates were community entertainment in those

years. Barney and the district schoolmaster, a Mr. Hughes, challenged Barney's father and older brother John. The subject of the debate was: "Resolved that the intemperate consumption of alcohol has been a greater evil than war." Bernard, Sr., was serving then as township treasurer and a school trustee. People liked him and his family. A crowd turned out to see the Caseys square off against one another to do battle with words and wits.[17]

Rebecca and Barney dated for some time after that. Barney completed his schooling and decided to return to Stillwater for work, though the couple agreed to exchange letters. For a short time, Barney had a job in Stillwater as a handyman and relief guard at the state prison. The environment was a bit unsavory and rough. Nonetheless, the young man was thrilled to meet the notorious Younger brothers, members of the Jesse James gang who were prisoners there. Before Barney left prison work, Cole Younger gave him a clothes trunk which Barney treasured.[18] Then Barney went to look for another job.

Barney worked hard and was well liked on the job. And yet, he just couldn't seem to settle down to anything he really liked. Finally, he found employment at a brick kiln in Stillwater. The other men working there, he soon discovered, were primarily of German backgrounds and had German tastes.

One day, when Barney had no lunch, one of his coworkers at the brickyard offered him an extra sandwich with Limburger cheese. Barney ate it but apparently did not think too highly of its strong flavor. "Have you ever eaten that kind of cheese before?" one of the men asked Casey later. "No, I never ate it," quipped the young Irishman, "but I've often stepped in it."[19] The German brickmakers roared with laughter. That young Irish fellow was all right, they agreed. But a strange and sad experience at the brick kiln later moved Barney to think more and more about his future. Was this kind of work what he was meant to do?

While he was at work at the kiln a few weeks later, a man

fell into a deep pit filled with water. Seeing that he couldn't swim, Barney jumped in after him. Soon, he found himself struggling with the desperate man at the bottom. Barney quickly realized that he could not calm or overpower the fellow in order to haul him to the surface. He could see that he was in danger himself because the drowning man would not release him.

For some reason, Barney grabbed for the brown scapular of Our Lady of Mt. Carmel which was hanging around his neck. His mother had given him the scapular a short time before. At just the moment he grabbed the scapular, he later told others, he felt himself being pulled up with the man in tow, seemingly by the scapular.

In the meantime, however, another man had jumped into the pit to relieve Barney. He could not get the drowning man to stop struggling and finally had to let him drown in order to save himself. Barney later believed that Our Lady would have saved him and the drowning victim through some miracle with the brown scapular.[20]

After this, Barney looked for another job. While still working at the prison, Barney heard that future jobs might be available with the new streetcar line Stillwater was planning. When he heard that there were finally openings, Barney Casey applied immediately. He'd been waiting for the opening. His heart was taken by the swift, sparkling contrivances. He was hired, trained as a motorman, and was soon working as a part-time motorman on Stillwater's electric trolley. He wrote to his family about his new work with great satisfaction.

Stillwater's streetcar system predated similar projects in most American cities. Young Casey was surely one of the first motormen in the country and possibly the youngest on the job. From the 1890s on, streetcar systems were to be found all over the country. They seemed to update a city, replacing horse-drawn cars, connecting towns together through interurban lines, and they were also inexpensive.

At some point during this period, however, Barney had received a disturbing letter from Rebecca. It may have contributed to his restlessness at some of his jobs. Enough affection had developed between Barney and Rebecca to prompt a proposal of engagement from young Barney. Marriages between seventeen- and eighteen-year-olds weren't so unusual in this era, and Barney was sure he could make a good living as a motorman in Stillwater.

In a return letter, Rebecca had informed Barney that her mother had refused her approval of the engagement. In the fall, Rebecca had added, she was to continue her studies at a boarding school in St. Paul. The letter was gleefully uncovered some weeks after Barney received it by three of his younger brothers. The boys had opened his suitcase during Barney's visit home. Whether it was clearly stated or spelled out "between the lines," Barney seemed to know that the relationship was ended.[21]

Just what effect this breakup with Rebecca had on the young man isn't clear. Barney was deeply emotional, as the Caseys knew, but for the most part, he concealed his feelings. As far as anyone could see, Barney continued to circulate generally among the young people of the area. For a while, he seemed to be attracted to Nell O'Brien. Later, Nell married his brother John. Barney seemed to enjoy the give-and-take of social mixing, but he remained a bit remote. And there did not seem to be a serious girlfriend in his life after Rebecca.

In mixed groups, the young man would grin, tell a few stories, and pull out his harmonica or the violin he had learned to play. His brothers, sisters, and his friends would laugh. Barney's playing wasn't good, but it was lively and he knew the latest tunes. Years before, during his first attempts at "scraping," his brothers had insisted that he practice his fiddle in the barn.

When a new motorman's position opened with a streetcar line in Appleton, Wisconsin, two hundred thirty miles away from "home," Barney took it. He seemed to want to get away, to travel a little farther from west central Wisconsin, which he knew so well. The Appleton job was good for a little while.

By 1890, however, Barney wanted to move closer to his

family again. He took a job with a streetcar line in Superior, Wisconsin. It was about one hundred twenty-five miles from the Caseys' homestead. After jumping from job to job, Barney had more or less settled into work as a streetcar motorman. Two or three years of experience still gave him a sort of "seniority" in this line of work. Streetcars were new, but they seemed to be a permanent addition to life in the city.

Though the Caseys were elated to have Barney closer to home, he couldn't really help with problems there. Drought and insects had devastated crops for several years in succession. When Barney, Jr., saw that there were plenty of jobs in Superior, he wrote to his family to tell them of the opportunities. It was 1891. American agriculture was suffering from a widespread depression.

Barney's three older brothers, Jim, Maurice, and John, moved to Superior almost at once. The four Casey boys rented a house together, and their sister Ellen temporarily quit her teaching position to care for the house and them. Barney wrote to his parents again and urged them all to come to Superior. Finally, that same year, 1891, the head of the family sold the Burkhardt farm to a real estate company in exchange for ten city lots in Superior.[22]

Before long, Bernard Casey, Sr., moved the remaining Caseys, family belongings, and all of the livestock north to Superior. A new farm was rented and the family was soon on better financial ground with their older sons working at good jobs in the city.

Bernard and Ellen built a ten-room house and were content. The three little girls — Margaret, Grace, and Genevieve — were enrolled in Sacred Heart Church's parochial school while the older Casey children began to attend high school. Even John, who was a year older than Barney, went back to school. Thinking of a profession as a lawyer, he took up the study of law during the evenings.[23] Life was settled and satisfying for the Caseys. Except for Barney.

One autumn afternoon in 1891, things began to take a different direction for Barney. He was at work and his streetcar was making its usual run. As he rounded a corner, the young motorman immediately spotted a cluster of people on the tracks ahead of him. He hit the brakes and the streetcar screeched to a halt. Barney and his passengers poured out to see what had happened.

Lying on the tracks in a pool of blood was a young woman. A drunken young sailor was hovering over her, cursing. The sailor was clutching a knife dripping with blood. As policemen pulled away the murderer at gunpoint, others lifted the woman's lifeless body off the tracks.[24]

Close to twenty-one years of age, Barney Casey, Jr., had lived most of his years on the farm among peaceable people. The dead body and the drunken words of hatred introduced him to something new, something sad and evil. The event was a shock to his psyche. Barney nevertheless gathered his passengers and went back to work. In some way, however, the young man began to brood about the senseless murder on *his* tracks.

Of the many sons of Bernard and Ellen Casey, this namesake son was one of the most introspective. Barney began to agonize about the direction of his own life. Since the broken romance with Rebecca Tobin, he had had few goals for his future. While the family still needed financial help, Barney put concerns about his own future aside. He felt obliged to help his family. But now the family was secure again. Old questions that had preoccupied him from time to time resurfaced.

Barney began to debate something that was deep in his heart. He'd done plenty of rhetorical debating in the past. This time, however, the exercise was not for fun. Ellen and Bernard, Sr., weren't sure what was going on inside the handsome young man. But Barney himself was finally sure. He went to see Father Edmund Sturm, the pastor of Sacred Heart Parish in Superior, to discuss the priesthood. Quietly but quickly, the inclinations of the young streetcar motorman began to move his life onto an entirely new track, into a new direction.

CHAPTER THREE

Following a New Direction (1891-1898)

When Barney went to talk with Sacred Heart Parish's Father Edmund Sturm, he knew only that he wanted to move in this new direction. He thought that he wanted to give his life to God in religious life as a priest. Beyond that, he had almost no ideas about the kind of ministry he wanted to do or the sort of seminary he should choose.

Father Sturm listened to the young man seated in front of him dressed in the trim, dark uniform of a streetcar motorman. He seemed to be a likable fellow. His slender build made him look taller, but Barney was actually an inch or two under six feet tall. Though the Caseys had only recently moved into his parish, the pastor had heard quite a bit about them. He was very impressed with the young man's parents, Ellen and Bernard, Sr. Superior was also impressed with the "Casey All-Brothers Nine," a baseball team comprised of the Casey brothers for which young Barney fearlessly played catcher.[1]

After listening to what the young fellow had to say, Father Sturm quietly suggested that Barney apply for admission to St. Francis de Sales Seminary in Milwaukee. This was the same "German seminary" where Barney's brother Maurice had been enrolled. His brother's attempt to study for the priesthood there had ended disastrously, Barney knew very well. Maurice had come home convinced that he was both a failure and a deep disappointment to his family. But Barney took Father Sturm's advice and made plans to follow the path Maurice had taken. He believed that this was the life God wanted for him and that God would move him toward this goal.

Barney stood up, shook hands with his pastor, and left. The anxious, heavy feeling that had been burdening him seemed to be gone. He walked out of the rectory and made his way to the streetcar station where he was to begin work within the hour. Later in the day, Barney smiled to himself, he would tell his family about the new track he would be taking.

At the Casey household, Barney's news was greeted with great joy. Ellen and Bernard, Sr., were almost speechless, but they had suspected that their Barney was thinking of such a move. Barney explained that he would have to enroll on the high-school level with fourteen-year-old boys. At that, fifteen-year-old Gus told Barney that he would be one semester ahead of Barney, who would begin in the middle of the school year. Barney was not really disturbed by such a prospect. In fact, he was eager to begin.[2]

Just a few months after the streetcar episode in Superior, Barney found himself in class again. It was January, 1892. Milwaukee was cold and snowy. Barney found himself in a different world, and this world was speaking a language he didn't really know. At dinner, during recreation, and in classes, young Casey found himself immersed in a German world. Barney may not have realized it, but St. Francis Seminary had been at the center of some controversy. The controversy was over ethnic bias — a common concern during these decades of immigrant settlement. Long before he set foot in St. Francis, the controversy had been brewing.

36

The diocese of Milwaukee had been founded in 1843, and the diocesan seminary had begun to enroll young men in 1856. Even in its first year, according to its rector, Father Michael Heiss, German and Irish Catholics were defensive about the seminary's direction.

"Some thought that the seminary would become an institution solely for the Germans. When, however, we also accepted Irish youths, certain parties spread the suspicion that it was planned to displace the Germans gradually and to make the seminary Irish."[3]

At that point, German worries were misplaced. The diocesan seminary began with a German staff and emphasis and remained that way for some years. The seminary staff was assigned by Bishop John Henni, the first bishop of Milwaukee, who had come with strong German associations from the diocese of Cincinnati. Nonetheless, it was true that the Irish clergy — both the native-born and foreign-born — were clearly trying to gain their own foothold in the German establishment.[4]

German clerics in Wisconsin undoubtedly felt that defensiveness about Irish leadership was justified. Over half of all Catholic bishops in the United States from 1789 to 1935 were Irish, even during decades when Irish Catholics represented only seventeen percent of the Catholic population.[5] German Catholics had a saying which expressed this fear: *Mit der Sprache ghet der Glaube* ("With language goes faith"). If they lost their right to worship in their native tongue and to teach their children that language, they feared that their children would lose the faith.

When Archbishop Henni was about to retire in 1878, both American and Irish priests began to write letters aimed at discouraging the appointment of another German. They wrote to Archbishop James Gibbons of Baltimore pointing out that in Wisconsin the archbishop of Milwaukee and the bishops of the other two dioceses, La Crosse and Green Bay, were German, as were all ecclesiastical officials. There had never been an English-speaking priest in any of these positions, they pointed out.[6] In spite of these efforts, Archbishop Michael Heiss, the German bishop of La Crosse, succeeded to the archbishopric in 1880, and was followed by another bishop of German background, Frederick Xavier Katzer, in 1891.

Barney Casey had therefore come to Milwaukee just about one year after the archbishop. While Archbishop Katzer was struggling with Irish-German sensitivities at the chancery across town, one of his newest seminarians was doing battle in the classroom.

This was a German seminary and German and Latin were required courses. To help pay for his tuition, Barney became the seminary barber. Since students rose at 5:30 A.M. and were required to follow a rigid daily routine, the barbering job took time away from needed study. Barney struggled to fulfill all of his obligations. It was in the academic arena that he began to understand the pains and frustrations that life can bring. Stress, and possibly the cold rooms in this five-story seminary near Lake Michigan, contributed to his frequent attacks of "quinsy sore throat."

Barney was well liked at St. Francis. Though quite a bit older than his classmates, he did not put himself above them in any way. Working very hard at his studies, he also took some time to do some skating on the big rink during the winter and to play some ball during the warmer months. When he assumed the role of catcher for the first time, he shocked his classmates.

Barney had always played catcher on the "Casey All-Brothers Nine" baseball team back in Superior. But to the horror of his young teammates and despite their appeals, he refused to wear a catcher's mask. With a quiet grin, the wiry young man simply made a huge sign of the cross in the air where balls would be zooming in and bats would be swinging at dangerous speeds. Then he crouched down on his haunches. To all who had come in contact with him, there was a deep spiritual quality about him. He was extremely and deeply prayerful, they noticed. But he was very approachable, too.[7]

Despite his busy schedule, Barney did extremely well at

his studies during his first semesters. The semesters of 1892, 1893, and 1894 passed in a blur of unceasing work broken only by some vacation and time spent with his family back in Superior. During the 1894-1895 school year, Barney was able to raise his grades high enough to enter the "fifth class," which was actually the first year of college seminary training. During the second semester of the 1895-1896 term, however, his grades dropped seriously. Seminary officials brought the young man in to talk to him frankly.

They told Barney they doubted he could do the academic work that further college-level seminary work would require of him. He had earned grades in the 70s in Latin, algebra, geometry, and history and in the 77 to 85 range in German. In vocal music, U.S. history, and natural philosophy, his marks had been in the 85 to 93 range. His grades in Christian doctrine and English had also been good, just as they had been during the first semester.[8] His marks were a bit low in some areas, but he clearly was not failing.

For reasons that he, at least, did not understand and didn't challenge, Barney was dismissed from the diocesan seminary. Bewildered, he prepared to leave Milwaukee believing that his journey toward the priesthood was suddenly coming to a halt. The diocesan seminary officials suggested that he might be more suited to seminary study in a religious order. They assured Barney that he did indeed seem to have a vocation.

Barney did go to visit the Capuchin seminary in Milwaukee. It was also called St. Francis Seminary. Once there, however, a great heaviness began to fill the young man, and he left the Capuchins quickly. The hint of austerity, the unkempt beards, and the somber setting at the Capuchin seminary depressed him. He headed home for Superior under a cloud that his prayers did not seem to lift. At twenty-five, and after four and one-half years of work, his dreams of serving the Lord were already dissolving, and he wasn't sure why.

In the months that Barney was still wondering why he'd been dismissed, an editorial appeared in the Milwaukee *Catholic Citizen*. The editorial writer noted that Wisconsin state colleges, Marquette College in Milwaukee and Sacred Heart College in Watertown, had all graduated a large number of Irish-Americans that year. But, the writer added, the graduating classes of Pio Nono College and of the diocesan seminary were composed entirely of German- and Polish-Americans. The *Catholic Citizen* challenge continued: "What is the explanation of the situation? Is there a dearth of vocations for the priesthood among the Irish-Americans of Wisconsin? Or is there something inhospitable about the atmosphere of St. Francis? We pause for meditation."[9]

It's likely that the editorial never came into Barney's hands. He was disturbed, but his feelings were more akin to confusion than to anger. He watched as his brothers pursued their goals. Jim had become a mail carrier, while Maurice had become a plumber and was traveling. John managed the dairy business for Bernard, Sr., while studying law. Ellen, his oldest sister and now in her early thirties, had recently married Thomas Traynor. Edward was in high school but was thinking about the seminary himself, while the younger children were still in grade school.[10]

In the throes of great distress, Barney's throat ailment recurred throughout the summer of 1896. His mother and sister Ellen tended to him and supported him in shouldering the pain in his spirit. The summer and autumn were seasons of torment for Barney. There were two matters that needed clarification in Barney's own mind, but he could not sort them out. The first was whether he had the call to the priesthood in the first place. The second question he needed to answer concerned the religious order he was to join in order to study again for ordination.[11]

On August 23, he wrote a letter to Father Bonaventure Frey, provincial of the Capuchins. They had already agreed to accept him *if* he decided to join them. Barney wrote:

> Dear Rev. Father:
>   I received your welcome letter of the 20th a few days ago. I would ask now what I should do with regards to

books, clothes, etc., as also when your scholastic year begins. I suppose you were informed about my bill of $525.00 at St. Francis. What should I do about that before I go to join you? — supposing I could not pay cash.

Hoping to hear from you again soon I am, very Rev. Father!

Yours sincerely
Bernard F. Casey[12]

Finally, toward the end of the year, after months of anxiety and prayer, Barney asked his mother and sister Ellen to join with him in praying a novena. He needed to have this matter of a vocation made clear. They readily agreed to his request and joined him in asking heaven for direction. The novena began.

On December 8, on the Feast of the Immaculate Conception, Barney was praying after receiving Holy Communion at his parish church, Sacred Heart, in Superior. The novena was almost over. On this day, a feast of the Blessed Virgin, Barney made a private vow of chastity. He decided that he would give his total devotion to God no matter what decision was made about religious life.

While Barney was praying during these quiet moments, he received a very distinct message in his heart. The message said: "Go to Detroit." Barney knew the meaning of that! It could only mean that he was to join the Capuchins, one of the three major branches of the Franciscan order. The Lord had been faithful and had answered his prayer. When he finally left Sacred Heart, Barney was feeling like a new man. His heart was filled with gratitude for the Lord's goodness. He jogged home to tell his family of his new call to the Capuchins. A little later, Barney found out more about the order he was to enter.

Established in Italy as a separate branch of Franciscans in the seventeenth century, the Capuchins had been named for the capuche, or hood, attached to their brown Franciscan robes. They had been founded by Matteo da Bascio and two others in the sixteenth century. Da Bascio's little band had been longing to follow the Rule of St. Francis "to the letter." Theirs was to

41

be a more strict observance and a life based on absolute poverty such as St. Francis had lived. The order quickly gained many members in Europe but was later diminished by plagues and political oppression. Around the time of its greatest decline in membership, in 1883, a Capuchin province was established in America with its base in Detroit.

The two founders of the Capuchin outreach to America were Father Francis Haas and Father Bonaventure Frey. When they came, these two were not even Capuchins. They were diocesan priests from Switzerland, but they had a commitment to the Capuchin charism. The two priests had arrived in America in 1856, the year before Barney Casey, Sr., arrived from Ireland. The Capuchin pioneers as well as Bernard Casey had been penniless and unsure about where their future would be in this land. In the years that Barney Casey, Sr., was founding a family and livelihood, the Capuchin founders were setting up missions in Wisconsin, Michigan, and near New York City.[13]

The Capuchin history was impressive, but Barney, Jr., contemplated it with mixed feelings. The message about going to Detroit was not a message Barney would have been likely to "invent" for himself. He had been uncomfortable at the Capuchin house he'd visited in late spring. It was quite formal and austere. The Capuchin monks wore beards in imitation of St. Francis, and this bothered Barney. Barney's own father had always worn a beard. But the Capuchins were to leave their beards untrimmed out of respect for the Franciscan call to simplicity. The thought of it did not appeal to Barney, Jr., at all. He was aware that his abhorrence of Capuchin whiskers was a minor factor. And yet, there was really nothing about the prospect of joining the Capuchins that appealed to him.

Nonetheless, by December 20, Barney was ready to "go to Detroit." Because it was so close to Christmas, his family wanted him to stay and spend the holiday with them. They knew that it would be years before they would see him again. But Barney would not yield. It was, he insisted, time to go.

In what proved to be a blinding snowstorm, he left Superior on December 20 and headed southwest for St. Paul on the 11:00

42

P.M. train. From St. Paul, his train then headed east, pulling along slowly through drifting snow to Milwaukee. After a brief layover there, during which Barney stayed with Capuchins for the first time, he boarded a train again. Down through Chicago and over to Michigan, his train headed for his goal — Detroit.

On Christmas eve, the train finally pulled into the station in Detroit. Barney located a streetcar and headed for Mt. Elliott Avenue. There, at 1740 Mt. Elliott, the young man finally arrived well after dusk. He was exhausted and refused the offer of dinner. Barney could see no farther than a bed at this point. Upstairs on the second floor, he was shown to his room: a simple, stark little room with a wooden door latch. The sight of it immediately renewed his fears of this Capuchin austerity, but thinking about it was just too much for the young man. Moreover, he was exhausted by the strain of travel and a difficult decision. Pulling off his shoes and his heavy coat still wet with snow, he hung the coat on a hook, got in bed, pulled a blanket up over him, and soon fell into a very deep sleep.

Just before midnight, he awoke to hear hand chimes and the voices of men singing. They were singing Christmas carols in German. It was Christmas Eve! As the voices grew louder, Barney could hear other men getting out of bed and coming down the corridor to join their voices with the little group of carolers. Barney joined them and his heart was lifted. The gloom over his decision to follow the Lady's orders and "go to Detroit" left him.

Down and around through the darkened corridors the carolers moved. Carrying candles, they were rousing the Capuchins who then followed them down into the chapel for Christmas Midnight Mass. It was a moving, joy-filled occasion. It initiated a week or more of festivities.

Before long, however, the same anxieties about his decision plagued Barney once again. The transition to the new year provided no fresh hope or renewed vision that his future here could be happy and fulfilling. Capuchins were invested with the habit very soon after entrance, but Barney seemed to dread the finality of that.

His investiture into the novitiate was set for January 14, 1897. The closer the date came, the more anxious he felt about his decision. Penning his thoughts into his small book on the Rule of St. Francis and the Constitution of the Capuchins, he referred to this day of investiture as a "day of anxiety," and its coming looked to him as "dark indeed."[14]

On January 14, however, Barney finally slipped the heavy brown cassock over his head and pulled on the Franciscan's heavy sandals over his socks. Perhaps he pulled some new vision or a feeling of peace over his psyche at the same moment. Whatever the reason, the actual investiture seemed to settle his spirit. Those painful anxieties and second thoughts seemed to dissolve into the wide, high hallways of the friary that he would come to know very well.

From the fourteenth of January, Barney Casey was known among the Capuchins as "Frater" (or "Brother") Francis Solanus Casey. St. Francis Solano, a Spaniard, had been a violin-playing Franciscan missionary in South America during the seventeenth century. Francis Solano had had a powerful gift of preaching and had taken the pains to learn so many of the local dialects that he was thought to have the gift of tongues![15]

In July, 1897, seven new men entered the novitiate program to join Frater Solanus and two other novices, Leo Steinberg and Salesius Schneweis. Life in the novitiate was rigorous but not completely new to the young man from Superior. For four years he had lived a very ordered life at St. Francis de Sales Minor Seminary. Because the new Frater Solanus had entered the Capuchin novitiate in January instead of in the summer as men usually did, he was between regular groups. Fraters Leo and Salesius were six months ahead of him in the novitiate and the seven new men were six months behind. The novitiate term of Solanus was to be longer because the vows ending the novitiate were made only in July.

Day by day, Solanus merged his life with the schedule of the friary. It was certainly different from the life he had come to know as a conductor on a streetcar line. In that life, he had kept his pocket watch handy to double-check the time. To be at the right intersection at precisely the right minute was important.

Inside the monastery, men walked, talked, ate, and slept in a pattern that was hundreds of years old. The proximity of the twentieth century changed life here very little. Living the monastic life, Solanus and the other friars were wrenched from sleep each day at 4:45 A.M. The youngest brother walked up and down the halls where the friars were sleeping in their rooms which were called cells. This "early bird" friar clapped two two-by-four boards together to awaken the rest of his brothers. After this harsh awakening, the friars then had fifteen minutes to wash a bit and don their brown habits and sandals before they went to the chapel.

Each friar's cell was simple and spare. That of Frater Solanus, like those of other Capuchins, was a room of about nine by twelve feet. In every cell was an iron bed with a cornhusk mattress and a pillow. The pillowcases and sheets were made from mattress ticking.[16] There was a window, but it had no curtain. A small table, a small armless chair, and two clothes pegs on the wall rounded out the "furnishings." There was no closet. Capuchin brothers could hang all the clothes they owned on those two hooks.

At 5:10 A.M., the day of prayer began with Lauds. The Litany of the Saints, private meditation, and the Angelus, said just before 6:00 A.M., prepared the friars for Mass, which began at six o'clock. At seven, breakfast was served in the refectory. It was simple — cereal or bread and coffee. It was eaten in silence. Any time remaining before 8:00 A.M. was used for spiritual reading. At eight sharp, the workday began.[17]

For the Fathers in Detroit, the workday might mean confessions, preaching missions at parishes, or officiating at funerals at Mt. Elliott Cemetery across the street from the friary. The Capuchin priests also officiated, when needed, at parishes around the city of Detroit on weekends.

The Capuchin brothers, also in residence at the monastery, shouldered the jobs of food preparation, making, repairing, and cleaning clothes, maintaining the building and grounds,

45

running the printing press, and performing some office jobs such as serving as doorkeepers and the like.

The novices — both the clerical novices and those headed for the brotherhood — had classes to attend during the day. The novices who hoped to be priests also had other readings to do. They had to learn to say and participate in the reading of the Liturgical Hours and they also helped a great deal with liturgical services throughout the year. For the novices, including Frater Solanus, there undoubtedly were letters from home, but the novices were not allowed visitors or to visit home during this novitiate period.

In the refectory, benches and narrow refectory tables lined the walls of the large room. Friars therefore sat on the benches with no one seated across the table from them. At noon, dinner was served during which one of the Fathers read aloud from one of the Gospels. Other readings were also taken from the life of a saint, some devotional work, or from one of the papal encyclicals. One priest would read for a while and then hand the reading on to the next. This reading during both dinner and supper emphasized that no time was to be given to aimless socializing. The rule of silence was therefore observed during the meal but was lifted for Thursday meals, Sunday meals, and feast days.

After the noonday meal, the friars spent a half-hour in recreation while the novices spent some time individually in their rooms. Still later in the afternoon, the novices spent time from three to five o'clock at manual labor. Generally, this was outdoor work, which gave the young men some needed fresh air and an outlet for stored-up physical energy. In the garden or inside the monastery in the kitchen or chapel, the novices were working under careful supervision.[18]

Back in the chapel, the whole community gathered to read the Liturgical Hours before supper. Then there was recreation time, followed by some private time and the Hours again. The day was ended at 9:30 P.M. At that point, all the friars were in bed following a full day of prayer, physical exercise, and — for the novices — classroom work and study.

If Frater Solanus was not always asleep just as his head hit the pillow during these long novitiate days, his thoughts turned to his novitiate experience and what he was learning about himself. Like the other Capuchins, he had been keeping a private notebook and recording his thoughts about his life at St. Bonaventure. It was the practice of keeping a journal. With the guidance of his novice director, Solanus was experiencing a growing understanding of his own personality and spirit.

In his journal, it is clear that Frater Solanus was struggling to purify his motives and his heart. He began to see that he operated out of a single-minded intensity in accomplishing tasks. There was certainly no moral or spiritual fault to this tendency. But it was accompanied, he came to see, by a leaning toward perfectionism that was too rigid — a spiritual scrupulosity. Gradually, he loosened up, learning to lean more on God and less on himself.

Solanus also discovered, through his journal and almost daily conversations with his superiors, how very emotional and impetuous he was by nature. He had been able to disguise or hide these traits a great deal, but they were there. Perhaps, in the context of a large, well-disciplined Irish Catholic family, such personality traits are invariably submerged or played down, especially in boys. Few of his fellow novices recognized these traits. From what they could see, Solanus was an understanding, considerate, friendly fellow who was very intent on growing in holiness as a Capuchin.

As hard as he was working at his studies, he was working even harder on himself. He understood that the purpose of the novitiate was not to remake him but to take the personality and gifts already there and to develop them further for service to God and others. That was the idea behind the disciplines of the monastery. Capuchin spirituality, or Franciscan spirituality, was attempting to clear away some of the clutter of self-interest and self-indulgence that almost naturally attach to men and women who live life as though it were a right and not a gift.

During this novitiate year, the young man penned in his

notebook a sort of plan of action for learning to love God. It reflected the analytical, precise side of his nature. But the five-part plan showed great spiritual maturity as well. The twenty-six-year-old counseled himself to adopt:

1. Detachment of oneself from earthly affections: singleness of purpose.
2. Meditation on the Passion of Jesus Christ.
3. Uniformity of will within the divine will.
4. Mental prayer, meditation, and contemplation.
5. Prayer: "Ask and it shall be given to you" (Matthew 7:7).[19]

As passing years revealed, the plan was not one that Solanus would outgrow. It was a good guide for a second-generation Irishman anxious to live a life of Christian spirituality in a German order in twentieth-century America. In fact, it was a good guide for any Christian to follow. The novitiate year increasingly showed that the spiritual promise of Frater Solanus would not be the thing to worry about. Again, as it had years before, his academic performance became the concern.

By the end of 1897, the Capuchin superiors had already noticed that young Casey struggled with class work. Perhaps it all related to the difficulty he still had with Latin and German. Some kind of mastery of these languages was a prerequisite for ordination within this religious order. It could also be that his problems were more general than the difficulty of coping with languages. The Capuchins who had been watching the young man were not sure.

The superiors discussed their reservations with him. That was necessary. In July of 1898, the novitiate period would be up. By then, it would be time to either accept or reject all the novices as Capuchins. If Solanus could accept the prospect of living out his life as an unordained Capuchin — simply as a religious — there would be no barrier to that. They simply weren't convinced that he could master the material necessary for a man who would be ordained as a priest.

As hard as he had worked, both at St. Francis de Sales Seminary in Milwaukee and now in Detroit, such news must have been a source of grief to Frater Solanus. He knew, too, how disappointed his parents and family would be if he could not be ordained. If he was bitter about the prospect of having labored in vain, he did not openly express it. Possibly he simply suffered with the news and then worked hard to apply his own guidelines to the situation — detachment, meditation on the sufferings of Christ, and conforming to the will of God.

The culmination of concern about his academic potential was a signed statement he was asked to make. He wrote it and signed it in the presence of his superiors on the day before he was to take his first vows of commitment as a Capuchin. The statement was put into the monastery record on July 20, 1898. Frater Solanus Casey wrote:

> I, Fr. Solanus Casey declare that I joined the Order of the Capuchins in the Province of St. Joseph with the sure intention to follow thus my religious vocation. Although I would wish and should be thankful, being admitted to the ordination of a priest, considering the lack of my talents, I leave it to my superiors to judge on my faculties and to dispose of me as they think best.
>
> I therefore will lay no claim whatsoever if they should think me not worthy or not able for the priesthood and I always will humbly submit to their appointments.[20]

Why was such an "attestation" asked of a young man who ached for ordination to the Lord's priesthood? Frater Solanus already understood very well that his superiors were not guaranteeing his ordination just because he was now professing his first vows within the order. Whatever the reason, it must have been a very difficult piece of paper to sign. Solanus believed that he had a vocation to the priesthood. With this statement, he was surrendering his own deeply felt call to the will of his superiors.

On July 21, the day after he signed the attestation, Frater Solanus made his first profession of vows along with the other novices in his class. Each man vowed and promised to "live in obedience, without property and in chastity'' (the official vow formula for Capuchin Franciscans). With such a solemn promise made kneeling in the presence of all the other friars, each man rose as a recognized member of the Capuchin order. A critical landmark in religious life had been passed.

After taking their vows, Solanus and the others in his class prepared to take the train for Milwaukee. There, at the Capuchins' St. Francis Seminary, the young men were to continue their studies for the priesthood. It was a place that Barney Casey had visited in the spring of 1896 after he had been asked to leave the diocesan seminary. He had not been impressed with the Capuchins or their apparent austerity on that day.

More than two years later, on an early August day in 1898, Frater Solanus settled into the friary in downtown Milwaukee. He now lived under the watchful eyes of sixty-eight-year-old Father Anthony Rottensteiner. Father Anthony directed the training and schooling of the seminarians. He had a reputation as a rigid taskmaster in and out of the classroom. The last leg of young Casey's journey toward priesthood was beginning, but it was to be more difficult than he could have imagined.

CHAPTER FOUR

A Capuchin Vocation (1898-1904)

It was hot on the train from Detroit to Milwaukee. But what more could be expected of a July day? Solanus and the other five novices watched the midsummer countryside pass by as the train dipped southwest from Detroit, down through the rest of Michigan, skimming the northwestern corner of Indiana, and then into Chicago. From there, the route headed north, hugging Lake Michigan all the way up to Milwaukee.

In a way, Frater Solanus mused to himself, it was the reverse of the wild wintry ride he'd taken to Detroit eighteen months earlier. The green fields he was looking at now had been filled with blowing snow then.

Solanus watched the world go by and stroked the dark beard which now covered his lower face. God was directing his life, he felt very sure, and he supposed God was directing his beard, too. When he thought about it that way, a beard and even difficulties could be seen as blessings. It was a line of thought that Frater Solanus had need of soon after his arrival in Milwaukee.

As he entered the training in formal theology in the fall at the Capuchin seminary in Milwaukee, the academic weaknesses of Frater Solanus were revealed rather quickly. He found philosophy extremely difficult. He wasn't failing, but the downward slide of his grades seemed to predict a trend.

It's likely that the struggle he was having was the same one as before. Textbooks were written in Latin. Class discussions were now conducted exclusively in German. Discussing complex theological realities in a language that was still quite clumsy to his Irish tongue may have been the root of his classroom difficulties.

Although he was sixty-eight years of age, the director of the Capuchin seminary in Milwaukee was an imposing man. Father Anthony Rottensteiner's new class of clerics had already heard a great deal about him through the Capuchin grapevine. He was very demanding, they had heard. By all reports, however, Father Anthony would also give struggling but sincere students every benefit of the doubt.

He was, as Frater Solanus and his classmates found, a block of a man with a large wiry gray beard. In the classroom, he was thorough but would sometimes phrase questions so that the answers would be relatively easy to see and deliver. His students discovered that this master scholar was more often than not trying to see beyond academic accomplishments into their spirits. For some time, Father Anthony had been observing young Casey rather intently. The qualities of Casey as a religious and as a man had impressed Father Anthony, even if the fellow's scholarly talents had not.

Anthony himself had been an extraordinary scholar in his homeland. When he had asked to join the Capuchins in 1867, the order saw it as an answer from heaven. Someone with Rottensteiner's academic brilliance was needed to oversee the education of seminarians. Father Rottensteiner himself had a longing for mission work. But his real mission eventually became guiding young Capuchins to ordination at St. Francis Seminary in Milwaukee.[1]

Father Rottensteiner was willing to shepherd Frater Solanus through the intricacies of theology discussed in German. Yet, Casey's difficulties could not be overlooked. The impressions the Capuchin superiors had received from the seminary officials at Milwaukee's diocesan seminary seemed to be more and more on their minds.

As they always had been, the spiritual qualities of Frater Solanus were obvious to all. His personality and disposition also seemed to assure that he would blend well in community life. Nonetheless, the academic problems were a mighty stumbling block. A man's personal holiness and gifts could not outweigh academic shortcomings when the priesthood was involved. In addition to ministering, a priest was responsible for interpreting profound and vital theological truths for others. There was very little room for a margin of error in ordaining a man to such a role.

In the autumn of 1899, a year into Solanus Casey's major seminary study, the Capuchin authorities prepared to take a long, hard look at the future of the young man from Superior, Wisconsin.

During the first three semesters of major seminary classes, Frater Solanus stood fifth in a class of six. Behind him and standing much lower academically was Frater Damasus Wickland. Ranked fourth, just ahead of Frater Solanus was another Irishman, Frater John O'Donovan. But unlike Solanus, John knew and spoke German fluently. In the school year of 1899-1900, the men in this class were taking dogma, moral theology, canon law, Scripture, and liturgy. With the eventual addition of Church history, these were the courses that seminarians were studying until the end of four years of seminary training.

The seminary grading system was a simple breakdown into four levels of academic performance: "1" was a "Good or Very Good" grade, "2" was "Average," "3" was "Passing," and "4" was "Failing." Though Frater Solanus managed to get through each semester with at least a "Passing" (or "3") average, he seemed to be hanging on to that by a shoestring.[2]

While the Capuchin students were doing battle with books inside Milwaukee's St. Francis Seminary, the world outside was welcoming the twentieth century. Britain's Empire under Queen Victoria stretched across the world into five continents. Pope Leo XIII was on the Chair of Peter in Rome and was recognized as one of the most intellectual pontiffs of recent history.

The Capuchin students heard fragments of global and national news but only as their superiors handed such bits and pieces on. Theirs was a closed world designed to focus attention on a rather narrow field — ordination and spiritual growth. Mail to and from the students was permitted, but, in general, visitors were not. Frater Solanus had already been the beneficiary of one exception to the rule regarding visitors. This was the occasion when, not long after his arrival, his brother John and John's new bride, Nell O'Brien Casey, had stopped to see him. The intervals of recreation were also rare.

To make Frater Solanus understand their dilemma, the superiors and faculty asked him to consider and sign another "attestation," or statement, concerning his eventual ordination. The statement, written in German, was undoubtedly very well understood this time by Frater Solanus. He read it and signed it on July 5, 1901.

The statement said:

> I, Fr. Solanus Casey having entered the Order with a pure intention and of my own free choice, wish to remain in the Order, and I therefore humbly ask for admission to solemn profession. However, since I do not know whether as a result of my meager talents and defective studies, I am fit to assume the many-sided duties and serious responsibilities of the priesthood, I hereby declare (1) that I do not want to become a priest if my legitimate superiors consider me unqualified; (2) that I still wish to be able to receive one or other of the orders, but will be satisfied if they exclude me entirely from the higher orders. I have offered myself to God without reservation; for that reason I leave it without anxiety to the superiors to decide about me as they may judge best before God.[3]

Solanus thereby put his name underneath a statement that put his life's hope into someone else's hands.

Just what did this do to a man who had witnessed his parents' yearning to see one of their sons ordained? What did it do to him after entering a German order against his own inclinations? How did he feel after he'd entered seminary training late, only to attend classes with much younger boys and find that ordination still might be denied? At this point, Frater Solanus was already entering his thirties. Since his twenty-first year, he had been struggling to become a priest.

In the journal that he kept for personal reflection, the theme of penance surfaced often in notations for these days. Though his grades edged up, it did not seem to make his ordination any more certain as far as Frater Solanus could tell.

Father Anthony Rottensteiner, director of the seminary, seemed to be sympathetically witnessing the struggles of young Casey. One day, he listened as other seminary teachers discussed ordaining the seminarians to the subdiaconate. Apparently, there was some objection to moving Frater Solanus farther along this road toward the priesthood.

Shaking his large head, Father Anthony disagreed. It's true that Casey's academic troubles were worrisome, he said. But there was something else that this quiet, slender Irishman had. "We shall ordain Frater Solanus," Father Anthony predicted, "and, as a priest he will be to the people something like the Curé of Ars."[4] But Frater Solanus had no such confidence about his eventual ordination.

Living in such anxiety, medical authorities now understand, takes its toll physically as well as emotionally. Sometime during his last years of studies, Frater Solanus began to develop eye trouble. With many hours spent in reading and at least some of it in insufficient light, it should not have been too surprising. His eyes began to really ache. Distressed already by living in a kind of limbo about his future, he became really intimidated by this new difficulty.

Emotionally, he may have felt panicky. His chances for ordination were already jeopardized by his lackluster performance in the classroom. Would there be any chance at all if his superiors thought that he might have serious eye trouble later on?

Because of this, perhaps Frater Solanus did not wish to publicly admit to all the trouble his eyes were giving him. But his journal notes for this period betray his fear. The pain of this eyestrain really scared him. But on top of that, he was humbled by the fact that a physical problem like this could so claim the attention of a man supposedly trying to abandon himself to God! That realization bothered him. The whole problem began to swirl around in his head.

After a while, however, Frater Solanus decided that he should change his attitude about his ailing eyes. It was apparently a true inspiration. He began to look at his problems in a more positive way, trying to thank the Lord for the blessings he had already received. This new approach was rewarded. "Thanksgiving for same, June 12," he wrote in his journal on that date in 1902. On the following day, he was able to pen, "Consolation on 13th, 1902." Several weeks later, he received minor orders.

Changing his heart, opening himself to let go of some of the worry, and placing his full trust in God were rewarded. Beneath the notes in his journal, a phrase began to appear more and more often: *Deo Gratias* — "Thanks be to God." It was becoming second nature for Frater Solanus to thank God for whatever life was to give to him.[5]

Father Anthony may have had some special gifts when it came to predictions. In February of 1903, the seventy-two-year-old seminary director fell ill. Knowing how he had loved his work with seminarians in the classroom, he had also once said that if he could not teach, he would die. Five days after he had taught his last class, he died.[6] Feeling a tremendous sense of loss, his seminarians struggled ahead without him.

Four months after the death of Father Anthony, Solanus was touched by another death. Opening a letter from home, he read that his first love, Rebecca Tobin, had died. She was thirty-three. Thinking of the death of the woman he nearly married made him wonder about the mysterious designs heaven creates. In his journal, Solanus wrote simply: "Today, for the first time in seven years, I heard about Rebecca. R.I.P. O queer world and uncertain."[7]

To the left of this note about Rebecca, he penned in "Deo Gratias." It was certainly not thanks for the death of a girl he'd loved. Frater Solanus was beginning to understand something very fundamental about God.

Through trials, illnesses, and even losses such as the deaths of Father Anthony and of his sweetheart from the past, Solanus could begin to see God's love and goodness. It took a special sort of spiritual vision to see love in life's tragedies and disappointments, but this seminarian, who'd been having trouble with his eyes, was developing the knack for it.

In February, 1904, the Capuchin superiors began to look again at the grades of Frater Solanus. It would be the last assessment of his academic standing. In the first semester of his last year of seminary work, his grades in dogma, moral theology, and canon law had improved. He had a passing grade in each of the three. Though he was not the only student with problems in Scripture and liturgy, the problems were serious. The three students at the bottom of the class were not even given grades in these subjects for this semester.

Anxiety over his ordination was hanging like a heavy gray cloud once again over his head. Solanus wrote to his oldest sister, Ellen, that although he would "probably be ordained a deacon and priest before August," he still had misgivings that it wouldn't happen. He also told her that he hoped the Holy Spirit would guide his superiors in their decision in all this. But the uncertainty must have been torturous. Instead of his name on this letter, Frater Solanus simply wrote the word "Resignation" with a little cross behind it.[8]

When the time came for a decision about the three men lowest in class standing, only a few months remained until the scheduled ordination in July. It was prayerfully determined that all six men in the class were to be ordained to the priesthood. Father Anthony's prophecy was already partially correct. Solanus was to be ordained.

Possibly because of his fluid familiarity of German, it was eventually decided that Frater John O'Donovan, the fourth in the class, would be ordained with full faculties. He could, after all, certainly hear confessions of German-speaking peoples who predominated in the areas that the Capuchins served. His academic average had been higher than that of the other two, but not by any great margin. There were some Capuchins who later believed that faculties had initially been withheld from John also, but that he had argued his case successfully for full faculties.[9]

Fraters Damasus Wickland and Solanus Casey, on the other hand, were to be ordained as *sacerdotus simplex*, that is, "simplex priests" (or "Mass priests," as they were sometimes called). They were truly and fully priests but were not to exercise the faculties of hearing confessions or preaching homilies for congregations. Such a decision was surely as painful for Capuchin superiors as it was painful to the two men. It was not a decision that was made quickly or casually. To have relatively young, healthy men ordained who could never really make a full pastoral contribution in a parish was a hardship and a loss to the Capuchin community.

Did Damasus and Solanus ever discuss their feelings about the decision with each other or with John O'Donovan? How did the Caseys — the parents, brothers, and sisters of Solanus — see this limitation on his priestly role? Such feelings are not recorded, but the loss was surely felt by everyone. There was one day, at least, in which these concerns were probably forgotten.

July 24, 1904, was the day that Solanus and his classmates had prayed for. In the vestibule of St. Francis Church in Milwaukee, not far from the classrooms where they had struggled, stood six bearded young men — Fraters Damasus Wickland, John O'Donovan, Fabian Fetha, Pius Stutzer, Maurus Ascherl, and Solanus Casey. They were about to be ordained by Archbishop Sebastian Messmer, the new bishop of Milwaukee.

"Father Solanus" fairly glowed with happiness that day. At thirty-three, he had finally reached a goal set a dozen years earlier at age twenty-one. He had been a streetcar motorman in Superior, Wisconsin, when the journey toward priesthood began. The Lord had put him on a new track and began to move him in a new direction on that day in 1891. If Solanus did not think about this vocation in terms of that sort of metaphor, it would have been surprising.

Exactly one week later, the brand-new "Father" Solanus was again in the vestibule of a familar church. This time, the church was St. Joseph's at Appleton, Wisconsin. A Capuchin regulation required a newly ordained priest to say his "First Mass" in the Capuchin-staffed church closest to his home. Though two hundred miles from the Caseys still living at Superior, Father Solanus joyfully spotted many members of his clan. Among his brothers, Jim, Maurice, and Edward were there. Of course, his parents were there, too.[10]

Solanus had not seen his mother, Ellen Casey, in eight years, not since the day he'd left in a blinding snowstorm to take the night train to Detroit to join the order. She must have found something different in the face of her now bearded son whose hair was already starting to thin on top. Surely, there were signs of a new strength, a new depth of spirit in this, her fourth son.

Though he was not aware of it at the time, Solanus later learned that his father had wept for joy through most of his namesake's first Mass. To think that one of his sons was now a priest. The reality was overwhelming for the sixty-four-year-old head of the family!

Maurice, at thirty-six, served at his younger brother's Mass. By then, Maurice was working for the Railroad Mail Service in Chicago and had come up to Appleton for the occasion. Later, in a private moment, Maurice drew his brother away from the crowd of proud family members and friends. Solanus wrote to his oldest brother, James, of the conversation years later: "Maurice . . . brought a tear to my own eye that day when the two of us were strolling in the Monastery garden. . . . 'By George, Barney, I think I'll have to try it over again. I'm getting tired of this blamed rail-roading!' "[11]

Though Solanus may have been amused at the lighthearted

way that Maurice confessed his plans to study again for the priesthood, he knew that his brother was serious about it. Solanus himself had only a little time to encourage Maurice and to spend time with his family. Within a day or two, he was to start out for Yonkers, New York. The first "Obedience" received by Father Solanus Casey didn't say very much. He was to be at Sacred Heart Parish in Yonkers and was to be there by August 4, 1904.

CHAPTER FIVE

A Priest and Porter (1904-1918)

On the first few days of August in 1904, a newly ordained Father Solanus Casey was on a train bound for the East Coast. His first assignment was to Sacred Heart Monastery and Parish in Yonkers, a suburb of New York City. He was to be there by August 4.

There had been no time to linger and relax in Wisconsin after his ordination and first Mass. He had to head east immediately. In fact, the journey itself must have been some small vacation for the thirty-three-year-old Father Casey. He was a former streetcar motorman. He felt comfortable with the back-and-forth jostling, the train's full-throttle rhythm.

The black-bearded Capuchin likely had his face to the window most of the way. He had never been east of Detroit. The state of Ohio, the Allegheny Mountains of Pennsylvania, the states of New Jersey and New York were all new to him. As the train rolled away mile after mile of his native Midwest, Solanus admired the farmers' fields. Harvesting was several weeks away.

It was the same good ground his parents may have crossed

in their journey west almost forty years earlier. They had come west to be settlers; their son Solanus was going east to the nation's largest city. New York was also said to be the second largest city in the world. Only London, with more than four million people, outranked New York City in size. It was not outranked in hustle and bustle, however. Turn-of-the-century New York was a vigorous city. New immigrants from Italy, Greece, and Eastern Europe were challenging the dominance of the Irish, Germans, and Scandinavians. With them came new ghettos, new foods, new ways. It was also a time of the Wall Street speculators and of opulence and conspicuous consumption for those lucky enough to inherit the fortunes of the previous generation's so-called "robber barons." It was the decade of the infamous sweatshops, too, culminating in the terrible Triangle Shirtwaist Factory fire of 1911. That fire claimed one hundred forty-six lives.

If the young Capuchin's eyes grew wide at the fertile stretch of Pennsylvania valleys, the city of New York must have seemed a miracle of twentieth-century life! Finally, he arrived. New York at the turn of the century was the showcase of American progress and political clout. For decades, Tammany Hall, a Democratic political organization, had heavily influenced New York politics. There was even a New Yorker, Theodore Roosevelt, in the White House.

Father Solanus could not take his eyes off the elevated trains in the city. With the elevated and the surface trains, this city carried more paying passengers during a year's time than all the steam railroads of North and South America together.[1] Solanus may have also noticed that the automobiles he saw were moving, stopping, and starting in a rather precise manner. Four years before, in the first year of the new century, New York had instituted its first traffic regulations, in spite of the outcry from "freedom-loving" New Yorkers.

His eyes may not have seen what was happening in the "bowels of the earth." For a nickel, however, New Yorkers were going mad over the newest form of traveling: the subway. Beginning at City Hall Station, to Grand Central, across

Times Square, to the end of the line at 145th Street, it was a great way to spend a day.[2] New York was also boasting of its remarkable new "skyscrapers." A building called the "Flat-iron Building" had been completed three years before, in 1901, in this city.

Making his way past these "big city" wonders, Father Solanus headed toward Sacred Heart Friary in Yonkers. Sacred Heart had been founded thirteen years before. Set atop some hills, the gray granite monastery overlooked the Hudson River. Solanus was happy to discover that his own sparsely furnished room had a good view of the river. The scene reminded him, he wrote later, of the rolling Mississippi and his early childhood near Prescott.

When Solanus was barely settled, he was summoned by the monastery's superior, seventy-three-year-old Father Bonaventure Frey. Father Bonaventure was fully aware of the unusual circumstances that Solanus presented to him. Bonaventure was the co-founder of the Capuchin order in America and had established Sacred Heart Friary and Parish.

In 1856, Father Bonaventure had come with Father Francis Haas from Switzerland. The two had almost no money between them. They struggled to establish monasteries, to found an American province, and had been successful. By 1883, the year St. Bonaventure Monastery was begun in Detroit, seven monasteries, most with parishes, had been founded in Wisconsin and New York.[3]

As Father Bonaventure contemplated the fine Irish features of Solanus Casey, he may have been thinking of his own life. Appearing before him now was a man, still quite young, whose apparent potential as an active Capuchin would be severely limited. Though he could and would perform baptisms and officiate at weddings, Solanus Casey could not really be assigned to Sacred Heart Parish. He lacked the faculties of preaching doctrinal sermons and of hearing confessions. With great kindness, Father Bonaventure finally told the newcomer that his assigned duties would be acting as sacristan and supervising altar boys in the parish.[4]

It may not have been until this day and this hour that Solanus Casey realized what his limited faculties would mean. In seminary days, he had dreamed of becoming a missionary. He could never be given a missionary assignment. With no bitterness and no brooding that anyone could note, Solanus graciously embraced his "assignments." Traditionally, such roles were not given to ordained priests but to the Capuchin brothers. Solanus had studied philosophy, canon law, dogma, Scripture, liturgy, and moral theology for ten years.

But very quickly, the friars noted, Father Solanus Casey had familiarized himself with the church and learned the locations and proper care of Sacred Heart's altar linens, priestly vestments, Mass articles, altar breads and wine, candlesticks, and flower vases. And he began to meet with the lively lineup of elementary schoolboys who were to serve Masses at Sacred Heart Church, which occupied the first floor of one wing of the friary.

Edward, one of the Casey brothers, wrote to Solanus when he heard the details of his older brother's first assignment. Always something of a poet, Edward put into verse his respect for Barney's humble acceptance of his tasks. He wrote a short poem called "The Brother Sacristan." In the poem, a "modest figure kneels to pay the voiceless homage of his heart" and then "silently from place to place he steals / the worship of his fingers to impart."[5]

Solanus treasured the poem. But he also treasured the chance to be in such close proximity with the Blessed Sacrament. He was very precise and devout in this role. A remarkable spirituality had been taking deep root in him for years. Here, in the work near the altar, it continued.

From another brother, Maurice, Solanus soon learned that the words about studying for the priesthood had not been carelessly spoken. Though almost thirty-eight, Maurice had located a seminary in Kitchener, Ontario.[6] Maurice said that he planned to try the seminary work and then join a religious order — perhaps the Capuchins — later. Solanus was delighted and knew that his brother Edward was also planning to become a priest. Three Casey priests! His father would be in his glory, Barney knew very well. Barney Casey, Sr., had always wanted at least one of his ten sons to become a priest!

Sacred Heart's young acolytes, on the other hand, often made Solanus wonder how his father had managed with so many boys. Solanus had the responsibility of drilling the altar boys to memorize the Latin responses at Mass. He also had to see that they showed up for Mass on time and piously performed their duties at the altar.

To get to know them and to win their trust, Solanus would often organize field trips for his gang of Mass servers. Ice-cream sodas always capped the trips, but visits to a church along the way were invariably included to "set a good example." Slender but wiry Father Solanus also impressed the boys when they played baseball together. Sometimes he would bat fly balls for them or hit them grounders to see if they were any good as shortstops.[7] When he played in a game, he was always the catcher refusing to wear the catcher's mask, and played in his habit. He played the game with gusto. The boys loved him for his wild courage and for his kind concern for them, too.

But despite their affection for him, Sacred Heart's altar boys groaned when they found themselves scheduled to serve Mass for Father Solanus. Slow with the Mass prayers and still cautious with his Latin, Father Solanus took more time with his Mass than any of the other priests. The Mass celebrated by Father Solanus seemed to take forever.

In 1906, a change took place at Sacred Heart that affected the assignments of Father Solanus. Father Bonaventure decided to retire. He was over seventy-five and was apparently becoming deaf and going blind.[8] He had worked long years in service to the Capuchin order and in dedication to the Church. He wished to simply live and work at the parish as any other priest. The responsibilities of pastor and superior of the house went to Father Aloysius Blonigen. Father Aloysius added to the mission of Father Solanus Casey. He told him that he was to take on the added task of being the friary porter.

In general, monastery porters were religious brothers.

Theirs was the daily "glory" of answering the doorbell, running for far-flung friars when visitors arrived, and handing on messages, packages, and occasional complaints. It was a job in which a porter might meet dozens of people each week. For the thirty-five-year-old Father Solanus Casey, the additional assignment was to have unforeseen blessings.

Sacred Heart Parish soon began to know "Father Solanus" in a new way. There were a half-dozen ethnic groups in the parish who spoke little or no English. But the porter's kind blue eyes and smile translated into every language. They saw him sweeping the sidewalks in front of the monastery and feeding the hungry who stopped there. And Solanus was invariably on the scene at Sacred Heart's traditional Labor Day picnic. It was easy to see that he loved the fun, the beer, the talk, and hot dogs with onions. He was an easy man to approach, and yet the priestly status of this very approachable priest didn't make any sense to many of Sacred Heart's people.[9]

It was known that he was a priest even though he did the jobs usually done by religious brothers. After visitors had confided in Solanus and had benefited from his easy counsel and prayers, they often asked him to hear their confessions.

"I can't do that," Father Solanus would respond softly. Instead, with little or no explanation, he would advise them to seek the sacrament from one of the other priests. Few if any of the folks in contact with the monastery would have heard of the term "simplex priest." A priest was a priest and did the things priests always do, they presumed.

With the exception of occasional *ferverinos*, or inspirational talks, Father Solanus, who seemed to be a deeply spiritual man, was not to be seen preaching at the pulpit. And he was never to be found hearing confessions at the church. No one outside of the monastery had any idea why. "Father Solanus loved God so much that he could not hear confessions. He might not be able to take it if he discovered how many people were hurting God!" That was the sort of comment being passed from one parishioner to another in the neighborhood.[10]

If the predictable patterns of priestly ministry were more

limited for Solanus Casey, other means of serving — extraordinary means — were not. Acting as porter, he opened the door, so to speak, to something very unexpected, something very good. "Favors" and "blessings" — that is what the youngish simplex priest called the events.

As early as 1901, even before ordination, Solanus had begun to record the circumstances of answered prayers. In part, this practice was mandated. Seminarians were expected to keep a spiritual journal.

Years later, after he was assigned to Sacred Heart, one of the notations Solanus made in this journal had to do with "altar boy trouble." In the long run, being distressed by sloppy service from boys may seem foolish. But for Solanus it was not foolish. Seeing to it that the boys served well on the altar was a good share of his priestly assignment.

Solanus Casey had decided years before that he was not going to do any part of his given jobs with less than one-hundred-percent devotion. A notebook notation finally recorded an answer to his prayer for better servers who would behave. Following a novena to the Immaculate Conception, concluded on December 8, the Feast of the Immaculate Conception, Father Solanus wrote, "Good boys asked to be servers!"[11]

A minor miracle? A small but happy coincidence? Solanus simply labeled all such occurrences and much more dramatic ones as "blessings." They all had one and the same name and came from one and the same source. That was the understanding with which he increasingly lived and worked.

A photo taken during this era *[see photo section]* shows Solanus posing with his charges in front of Sacred Heart. Twenty-six serious-looking boys, immaculately attired in surplices and cassocks, stand at attention with their director Father Solanus and with Father Anscar, the superior.

As the Sacred Heart porter, Solanus had begun to meet more and more people. There were Germans, Irish, and Italians. Many of the Italians were newly immigrated and needed an understanding friend, though Solanus would send for an interpreter in order to "understand" them. When they called for him or referred to him, Father Solanus Casey was "the Holy Priest."[12]

When visitors talked with Father Solanus, they apparently found nothing really remarkable in what he said. In fact, he was remarkably low-key. Solanus would welcome them and then invite them to be seated with him in one of the small parlors. Mostly, Solanus simply listened. Then he would close his eyes or look off into space as if to see into the issue more deeply. Only after the contemplation and quiet discernment would the bright blue eyes focus once again on the troubled individual seated in front of him.

The counsel that so many found comforting was inevitably very simple. He would ask them a few questions, pray with them, and finally suggest that they thank God for blessings already received and those they would receive in the future. Also, Solanus would often suggest that his visitors show some sign of gratitude for the Lord's goodness.

He would ask for more frequent use of the sacraments, especially penance and the Eucharist. Solanus would quote Pope St. Pius X, the great patron of frequent reception of the Eucharist. And sometimes he would ask if those seeking prayers would like to support the Capuchins' Seraphic Mass Association.[13]

"The SMA," as the Capuchins dubbed it, had been established about 1900 as a result of a Swiss woman's inspiration. Desiring to help the Capuchins, she suggested that the association might solicit donations for their foreign missions with the promise of remembrance through prayers and Masses. The Capuchins in the U.S. therefore promoted the SMA at each friary. In general, however, there was little aggressive promotion and, as a result, only minimal donations.

But after Father Solanus began to answer the doors at Sacred Heart in 1906, SMA donations coming in from Yonkers started to grow quite steadily. He said little about it, but his visitors gradually talked. They talked and talked about their prayers, the SMA commitment, and the fact that their prayers were being answered! In fact, prayers began to be answered at a rate which gained attention. Solanus had more and more requests to visit the sick down in the valleys.

Years later, a Sister of St. Agnes, Sister Agrippina (Carmella) Petrosino related that, as a young girl, she acted as translator for Solanus. She lived in the Italian neighborhood within the parish. On one occasion, Carmella's mother sent her to get Father Solanus for a woman who'd become ill soon after delivering a child.

"As soon as Father came in, he asked for holy water," Sister Agrippina remembered. "But they had no holy water. Father Solanus said, 'Oh, poor, poor, poor.' I ran over to our house and got some. When I came back, he prayed over her, blessed her and from then on the woman got over her infection and lived a long time afterwards."[14]

On another day, an Italian woman who knew Mrs. Petrosino, asked her to have her little girl bring Father Solanus. The woman had suffered from severe headaches for years. When he arrived, the woman asked Father Solanus to simply place his hand on her head. He did that as he recited some prayers from a prayerbook. The woman apparently got better, Sister Aggripina theorized, because she never again sought help from Solanus.

While walking along with his young Italian translator some time later, Father Solanus asked the girl what she hoped to be when she grew up.

"I'd like to be a Sister of St. Agnes," she told him.

"You will be," Father Solanus assured her with a smile.[15]

Even the girls who were already serving as Sisters of St. Agnes paid attention to the remarks Father Solanus made about the future. The nuns told one another that "if, in June, when you go back to the Motherhouse in Wisconsin, Fr. Solanus says, 'See you in September,' you will be coming back; if he just says 'Goodbye,' you will be transferred."[16]

Solanus Casey, his fellow friars noted, seemed to grow more assured about many things. The thing he seemed most confident about was the unending and boundless love of God. When Solanus did have the chance to give small *ferverinos*, it was usually for the groups he helped to direct at Sacred Heart.

Before addressing groups, Solanus prepared diligently. He always loved to write, and he was a very effective writer. English and composition had been his best subjects during school days. Pages of notes and jotted scraps of ideas would fill notebook pages before he finally wrote his talks. When the little homily was done, the message typically touched on God's love for his children. It was the first fundamental in the spiritual consciousness of Solanus. Learning to accept that love and respond to it, in his eyes, constituted the challenge of Christian life. His messages to groups or individuals seen in counseling were seldom more complicated than that.

In 1910, Solanus had the chance to repeat some of those themes for a special friend. Paul Francis Wattson, an Anglican, had founded an Anglican community of friars based on the Franciscan rule at Garrison, New York. It was about twenty-five miles north of Yonkers. Solanus met him and encouraged him. Finally, Wattson converted to Catholicism and studied for the priesthood. His religious community, the Friars of the Atonement, followed his path. Paul Wattson was so impressed with Solanus that he chose him to preach the homily at his first Mass on July 3, 1910.[17]

Toward the end of the year, Father Solanus made note of his fortieth birthday with a reference in his journal. There was no other recognition of it, with the possible exception of greetings from the family. Celebrated instead was the name day, the feast of the saint whose name the friar had received at investiture. Besides, due to a clerical error made when he entered fourteen years earlier, the birthday of Father Solanus was figured as October 25 rather than November 25.[18]

> November 25th '10, (40 Anniversary)
> Birth Day Present and surprise after
> long drought a gentle though copious Rain
> & after, beautiful Thanksgiving-Day, Deo Gratias[19]

In June of 1911, Father Solanus traveled to another ordination. Maurice was being ordained in St. Paul, Minnesota. He could remember seeing Maurice leave home to go to the seminary the first time in 1883. He had been thirteen and Maurice sixteen. Solanus rejoiced that his brother's dream was now finally fulfilled in the Lord. At ordination, Maurice was forty-three years old.

Two years later, Solanus traveled much farther to join in a family celebration. In the fall of 1913, Ellen and Bernard Casey, Sr., marked their golden wedding anniversary. Their ten sons and four daughters decided to gather together to celebrate the joy and fruitfulness of their parents. But the gathering had to take place in Washington State. In the early years of the century, six of the Casey boys had moved west as had Ellen, the oldest child, and her husband. With so many of their children in the Seattle area, the parents soon followed.[20]

Solanus went to talk with the superior of Sacred Heart. He asked permission to travel across the country. Travel from New York to Seattle covered 3,025 miles. With a week-long celebration also set aside for the October 6 anniversary and another week needed for the journey back, he explained that he would have to be gone for the better part of a month. Permission was quickly given. Father Solanus had been faithfully serving at Sacred Heart for nine years. Some other friars would answer the door, shepherd the altar boys, lay out the altar linens each day, and meet with the groups Solanus served as chaplain.

And so, on an autumn day in 1913, Father Solanus hiked his street-length cassock up a bit and stepped up into a passenger train. The black-bearded, brown-robed Capuchin drew plenty of curious glances as he made his way down the aisles. He smiled to the right and left and greeted a few folk. Solanus had little luggage and settled into a seat quickly. The longest sightseeing trip of his forty-two years was beginning.

Making the long cross-country journey was exciting for a man who'd never traveled much west of the Mississippi River. Across the Plains states, through the Rockies, up through the northwest to Seattle, Solanus thoroughly enjoyed the scenery as well as the people he met and spoke with along the way. But he looked forward most of all to spending time with his family. He had not seen his parents in years.

Since his move to New York, Father Solanus had had little time to talk to his two brothers who had been ordained. Edward, younger than Solanus by nine years, had been ordained at thirty-two in 1912, the year after Maurice had become a priest. All three brothers were to have a role in the Mass that marked their parents' anniversary. Father Solanus was to give the homily.

In Seattle, surrounded by their children and grandchildren (thirty-four in all), Bernard, Sr., and Ellen rejoiced in the blessings their fifty years together had brought.[21] It was the theme that their son Father Solanus was to use as well.

In the anniversary homily, Solanus spoke to all of the gratitude that should be given to God for past blessings to his mother and father. The joys and challenges of his parents' lives on their Wisconsin homestead were woven through his remarks. He pointed out that it was also good and just to thank God at any given moment for blessings to be given in the future. Father Solanus made it clear to the family that even hurts and illnesses were therefore properly viewed as blessings. Through the burdens of life, as he had learned in his simplex priesthood, God works his will.

It was a message that apparently touched his parents and his brothers and sisters deeply. They spoke of it at length. There were some tears. They saw in this son and brother a deeper and deeper faith. There was a spiritual gift that had been growing in the years during which he had been living so far from them all.[22]

If the joy of the reunion week was great, the pain of separation also loomed large. The Caseys realized that no other occasion could gather them all together again. There was time to talk, to play, to eat, to reminisce. When the festivities were over, Solanus boarded a train once again and headed east, back to New York. He had a commitment to Sacred Heart Parish.

In 1913, the parish was dedicating its church. Previously, the members of Sacred Heart had met and attended Mass in one of the first-floor wings of the friary. Solanus knew he should be back to see the new structure dedicated. And he longed to be with his parish for the event.

With tight travel scheduling, however, there was a great danger that he would miss the dedication ceremonies. But somehow, Father Solanus knew that he was meant to celebrate the parish event just as he had been able to celebrate his family's reunion.

On the way home, Solanus wanted to offer Mass at a parish church in St. Paul, Minnesota. But as the train pulled into the city, the conductor shook his head at the slender priest's inquiry. The conductor told Solanus that the only train headed for Chicago would be leaving within thirty minutes. He would have to stay in the station if he expected to be on it. Solanus needed to be on that Chicago train if he was to be home in Yonkers on time . . . at least in theory.

Father Solanus also knew in his heart that he should say Mass on this fall Friday morning. Leaving a puzzled conductor behind him and grabbing his skimpy suitcase, he left the train and walked off in a light rain to St. Mary's Church. There, he offered his Mass with the same conscientious care and attention that he always took.

When he arrived back at the train station, Father Solanus found that his Chicago-bound train was only then chugging into the station. It had been delayed. In Detroit, he repeated the "risk" to say Mass at St. Bonaventure's where he had entered the Capuchin novitiate. Back in New York, Father Solanus rejoined his parish in its celebration. To the joy of many there, he had arrived back in time to see it all through.[23] The Italians, Irish, and Germans who made up the people of Sacred Heart Parish knew that their celebration would be complete. Solanus was clearly a gift to the community and his presence made this family gathering a full one.

In 1914, Father Solanus had already completed ten years of service to Sacred Heart in Yonkers. In that decade, his gifts for relating to the troubled and the sick had been emerging. His ministry seemed to begin by answering the door and greeting visitors. But as the years passed, he seemed to hear a call to move out of the friary and knock on doors himself. Offering friendship and prayers for those who were bedridden or in pain, Father Solanus began to make it a habit to call on parishioners. He would carry holy water and a crucifix with him. He made special efforts to reach out to those of other faiths, especially Jews and Protestants. It was an unusual gesture for the day, but Solanus had carefully observed this ecumenical effort in Father Stephen Eckert in 1904, the year the two had lived together at Sacred Heart.[24]

In 1914, the world at large was on the edge of World War I. In late June, the archduke of Austria, Francis Ferdinand, and his wife, Sophie, were assassinated. Declarations of war followed within weeks: Germany, Austria, Russia, France, Britain, and Italy were among those declaring war. In the Vatican, Pius X had spent his spirit and his summer trying to reestablish peace. His efforts failed, and the seventy-nine-year-old pontiff died on August 20. Soon after, Pope Benedict XV came to the Chair of St. Peter.

In New York the military stretched a steel net across the narrows of New York Harbor to prevent German subs from entering. The city's German-Americans also suffered from anti-German sentiment.[25]

Radio and telegraph had begun to speed the news of world events. War talk spilled over into Yonkers, into Sacred Heart Parish. There were many newly immigrated people from Germany and Italy. Irish immigrants, as well, often had strong feelings about the conflicts because of a widespread hostility toward Britain. And so, new needs for healing and reconciliation continued to draw Father Solanus.

The pain being felt in Europe was compounded for the Caseys by the news that the head of the clan was ill. Bernard James Casey died in 1915 in Seattle after a lengthy and painful illness. He had died, Father Solanus was later told, saying a prayer to Our Lady of Sorrows. He was in his seventy-fifth year. There was, at least for Solanus, no time to go across the country to attend the funeral. He prayed for his father — and his mother — at Sacred Heart. Solanus then sat down and wrote letters of consolation to his mother.

Many letters, postmarked from Yonkers, were also going during this time to Maurice — or Father Maurice Joachim, as he was now called. Soon after ordination in 1911, he had been assigned as pastor for a massive mission territory in Montana. His mission, under the jurisdiction of the diocese of St. Paul, included eleven tiny parishes. One hundred miles separated the parishes at the extremities of his mission area. In between and surrounding them was breathtakingly beautiful scenery, though it seemed to matter very little to Father Maurice Joachim.

His brother, Solanus knew well, was not happy in his ministry. Edward had written to Solanus about it. Longing for the companionship and the bustle of the city, their older brother grew more and more morose. Solanus tried to share his vision of finding joy wherever God placed him, but Father "Maurice J." continued to suffer from despondency of one sort or another.

On the third day of January in 1916, Father Solanus wrote to his sister Margaret that he was still having trouble throwing off a severe chest cold. "I must try and answer your pleasant letter and beautiful boquet [sic] received this morning with one from Leo also. . . . Not that I am exactly sick, but I've had a touch of le grippe these few days with quite a cold in the chest and head. The latter cold seems softer since reading these letters. . . ." The chatty note went on to refer to the view of the Hudson which he had from his room and to his happiness with his vocation and work there in New York despite his inability to see more of the family. The letter was not mailed until two days later when Solanus added to it and sent it off noting that he'd fallen asleep before finishing it and later had been too busy to get it into the mail.[26]

In the spring of 1918, Ellen Casey developed pneumonia in Seattle. Letters from the "western Caseys" told Father Solanus of their mother's failing health. Fathers Maurice Joachim, from Montana, and Edward, from St. Paul, traveled west to see her. For Father Solanus, however, the trip was out of the question.

Ellen Murphy Casey could not relinquish her role as mother even during her last days. When Edward walked into her room, she asked him, "Father Edward, did you have any supper?" On May 2, Ellen Murphy died at the age of seventy-four. She had died surrounded by many of her children, including Fathers Edward and Maurice Joachim.[27] An influenza epidemic had taken thousands of lives during this last year of the First World War.

In June, Solanus made a notation in his notebook about an added responsibility at Sacred Heart Parish. "June 16, 1918. Today appointed and permitted to be 'Director of League' (after trying at least, to direct it for about ten years. Deo Gratias!)"[28] It was a privilege to officially direct the Sacred Heart League, according to Father Solanus, even though he had already been performing the service for ten years. The "privilege" was short-lived.

Several months after his mother's death, Solanus learned that he would be leaving Sacred Heart. A triennial chapter in Detroit had worked out assignments for the entire province. On the day he learned of the change, he was already packing to leave.

"I am just about to leave Yonkers for a new field, down in the very heart of the metropolis," he wrote to his sister Margaret on July 16. "In a way I almost feel sad to leave the Sacred Heart Monastery and Parish where I've been laboring (if laboring is the right word) for close to fourteen years. Well now, 'Goodbye' for the present from Yonkers. My new address will be 213 Stanton Street, New York City, New York."[29]

His new assignment was to be at the Capuchin parish called Our Lady of Sorrows. Probably the sting of leaving was blunted by his transfer to a parish dedicated to the Mother of God. In his long years at Sacred Heart, his boyhood devotion to the Blessed Mother had simply grown wider and deeper. He said his daily Rosary with great devotion and advised others to do the same.

A book called *The Mystical City of God* by Mary of Agreda, a Spanish mystic, also had a powerful impact on Father Solanus during his Sacred Heart years. He read it some years after arriving at the parish. In the book, the writer described the "life of Mary." Father Solanus found it a rich source for contemplating Mary's role in salvation.

The work had mixed "reviews" within the Church. Rome questioned the author's views about the truth of her work. Anyone who denied its contents committed a sin, she claimed. Because of statements like that, Pope Clement XIV stopped her beatification process in 1771. The work was condemned ninety years earlier due to some statements which theologians saw as extreme. Despite criticism of her written work, Mary of Agreda was acknowledged as a woman of great holiness.

Father Solanus knew of this controversy. He also was aware that *The Mystical City of God* was treasured by many churchmen in his own time. He saw the work primarily as a tool of inspiration and devotion. He had begun to regularly recommend it to people who came to him for spiritual counseling.[30]

Packing his few clothes, several books, a rosary or two, some pens, and his violin, the forty-seven-year-old Father Solanus tucked Margaret's letter into his pocket to mail later. Soon, he was investigating the streetcar schedule to make his way south to Manhattan. He said a quick good-bye to Sacred Heart, though few there yet knew that they were losing the Capuchin whom the Italians unabashedly called their "holy priest."

CHAPTER SIX

An Outbreak of 'Special Favors' (1918-1924)

Father Solanus Casey had no problem finding his way downtown into Manhattan and over to Our Lady of Sorrows at Pitt and Stanton Streets. He also knew that he would surely find his way in whatever new ministry his new superior would give to him. Our Lady of Sorrows Parish was well established. It had been founded in 1867 and the Capuchins were at home here.

Nonetheless, Solanus could not help but think of what he had left behind. He had been at Sacred Heart for fourteen years. He had moved through his first years of priesthood, through his thirties and into his forties. The tasks and responsibilities had grown throughout his years there. He had made friends in Yonkers and many people found a friend in him.

On this July day in 1918, Solanus found himself at a new door and at a new beginning once again. He rang the bell at Our Lady of Sorrows and waited for some brother Capuchin to open it. That was a task he had done so many times himself at Sacred Heart. But as he waited, he may have wondered what tasks were already being set aside on the other side of the door for a middle-aged simplex priest.

Father Solanus quickly learned that his days here at Our Lady of Sorrows would be less regimented. He was not given the job of porter. He was to act as director for the parish altar boys again. And, he was also given the role of moderating the Young Ladies' Sodality.[1]

As Father Solanus Casey settled into life in Manhattan in those early autumn weeks, the First World War was drawing to a close. Though American troops had only entered the war in 1917, more than seventy-five thousand U.S. service personnel had been killed. In addition, more than two hundred thousand had been wounded, were missing, or were prisoners of war. Two million American men had been sent to France while another two million had been in training in the U.S. when the Armistice ending the war was signed on November 11. Peace would return to the world, though Father Solanus and thousands of other Irish-Americans were concerned about the state of affairs in Ireland.

For Solanus personally, however, there was a new opportunity for peace. Without the responsibilities of counseling people, he was left with more time to spend quietly. He chose to study Scripture and to read more diligently. The Fathers of the Church, the lives of the saints, and the writings of the mystics were read or reread. Books were stacked up in his small room. Notes on what he was reading began to fill up his notebooks. In what could have seemed to be an embarrassing lack of "real responsibility" or "real work," he saw an opportunity to grow spiritually. And this kind of growth took time.

During the months that followed, Solanus would frequently make his way to the monastery chapel to pray in the presence of the Blessed Sacrament. Contemplation had always been a favorite form of prayer for him. But now, because he was reading and studying more about it, he was even more attracted to it. He read and reread the works of St. Catherine of Siena, St. Bernard, and others. In addition to the powerful silence and prayer he was reading about, a powerful exchange was apparently continuing and deepening between Father Solanus and his God.[2]

Outside the friary, New Yorkers were discussing the "hot topic" of 1920. That was the newly ratified Eighteenth Amendment to the Constitution (more popularly known as the Prohibition Amendment), which outlawed the manufacture, transportation, and sale of alcoholic beverages. Some German-Americans in the city were sure that the amendment was a cleverly concealed plot to persecute them. By and large, Germans owned and ran the nation's breweries.

Sometime in 1921, the monastery journal reported that Father Solanus was hospitalized at St. Francis Hospital. Up to this point, there had been few notations of any kind about him or his three years of ministry at Our Lady of Sorrows. It was almost as though his presence there was a secret. Solanus had developed some kind of gangrenous infection which quickly became painful and dangerous.

He had to be admitted to St. Francis Hospital. At fifty, he was operated on for the first time in his life. The emergency surgery took place on a Sunday morning after Father Solanus endured a night of excruciating pain. When it was over, Solanus wrote about the illness in a letter to his sister Margaret LeDoux in California.

"I had been in agony for at least 40 hours though no one seemed to know it," he wrote. "While I tried to thank God for it all, my principal prayer — at least a thousand times repeated — was 'God help us.' " Only as he came out of the anaesthetic and dimly saw that the doctors were completing his work could he again pray, "Deo Gratias! Thanks be to God!"[3]

It was a lesson in pain and helplessness that probably could not have been provided to an individual without this sort of personal suffering. As the ordeal concluded and his infection and pain receded, Solanus thanked God again and again. He was leaving the hospital after a short stay. But he was even happier that he had been able to say Mass every day, even during the most painful hours.

Later in the same year, on October 21, 1921, Father Solanus learned that he was being transferred again. This time he was to move to Our Lady, Queen of Angels Parish (sometimes simply called Queen of Angels Parish or Our Lady of the Angels Parish), which was located in Harlem. It had been a three-year assignment at Our Lady of Sorrows. It had been a quiet three years. The monastery log at Sorrows noted on October 25 that Father Solanus Casey was going to Queen of Angels while a Father Cajetan was coming from Harlem to Our Lady of Sorrows.[4]

It was an even exchange of men. As usual, there was no explanation for the change of assignment. Assignments were a matter of obedience, not discussion. On the same day he learned of his transfer, Solanus packed up and headed for 113th Street and Third Avenue in Harlem.

If Father Solanus expected to continue with the same ministries at his new parish, he immediately discovered that there were changes planned for him. At Queen of Angels, he was told he was not to act as sacristan, director of altar boys, or chaplain for the Young Ladies' Sodality! Solanus, who was not quite fifty-one years old, was to have only one assignment there. But this assignment was to be a demanding one.

At Queen of Angels, Father Solanus was to spend all of his time in pastoral work. That was to be his real role, though he was given the title of monastery porter to assure his easy and constant contact with people in need of help. He was also to be the promoter of the Seraphic Mass Association.[5]

Obviously, the work that Father Solanus had done years earlier at Sacred Heart had made an impression on the provincial superiors. Perhaps the time given to him at Our Lady of Sorrows was intended to test him. Or maybe it was given to provide him with an opportunity to deepen his spiritual roots. Capuchin superiors knew very well that a man who was restless for the daily dynamics of meeting and counseling people could not be well grounded in spiritual realities.

Solanus, on the other hand, had rejoiced in his quiet time, the time for prayer given at Our Lady of Sorrows. There was no chafing under his enforced assignment to "inactivity," to silence. He grew because of it. He rejoiced in the opportunity for quiet prayer, reading, and study. That was easy to see.

The truth was that the province of St. Joseph had never seen a Capuchin quite like this soft-spoken, Wisconsin-born Casey. His superiors knew that he would have to be guided under the vow of obedience by which he was bound. And yet, it was also clear that great gifts operated through him. Those gifts, they knew, should not be quenched. God seemed to want to operate in a special way through this man whom they had ordained with only limited faculties.

So, the new porter settled in and began to answer the door at Our Lady of the Angels. A front office was provided for his use. People who came to seek his help typically wanted to talk for a while. In a very natural and quite spontaneous way, Solanus began to see and counsel people all day long. No appointments were made. People simply came, lined up inside and outside of the front office, and finally poured out their problems to him. There was nothing different in the way Father Solanus was now handling those who came to him. The approach was the same one that he had used at Sacred Heart.

On his desk, Father Solanus had a book for enrollment in the Seraphic Mass Association (SMA). When he thought it was appropriate, he would ask those seeking answers to receive the sacraments more often or to seek God more enthusiastically in prayer. He also often asked if he could enroll them in the SMA. He was an official promoter for the Seraphic Mass Association and he believed in it completely. By asking for participation in the SMA, he was actually trying to draw out some sign of expectant faith.

That seemed to be crucial for him. If the petitioners would agree to commit themselves, he would methodically enroll their names, addresses, and intentions in careful, legible script in the SMA enrollment book. As at Sacred Heart, the book began to fill. The usual charge of fifty cents for annual enrollment was collected unless Solanus could see that it was a hardship to ask for it.[6]

Through the autumn and winter of 1921 and into the new year, the pattern and the procedures continued more or less unchanged. The people came with troubled marriages, threats of dangerous surgeries, estranged children, dying mothers, needed jobs, or alcohol-related problems in this era of Prohibition. There were literally hundreds of concerns to take to heart and to take to prayer.

Solanus seemed to handle each need, each set of worried eyes, delicately but effectively. He radiated a sense that God cared about all those things. He often laid hands on those who were sick and prayed for a healing then and there. And his promises of prayer for individual intentions were more than polite promises. He began to spend hours and hours in the chapel after office hours and his Capuchin house commitments were fulfilled.

As the weeks went by, many people began to return to the monstery with a certain lift in their step, with a light in their eyes. They waited in line for their turn, interspersed among worried and weary petitioners. They came to tell the slender porter that there had been a healing, a reconciliation, a job placement, a miracle! Prayers were being answered.

Father Solanus would listen to the good news. He rejoiced in the joy of prayers being answered. His blue eyes would light up above a smile wreathed in his graying beard. But, invariably, he reminded his happy visitors that thanks were due only to God, only to the prayers and intercessions of many Capuchin priests who had remembered their intentions in Masses. He would urge a continuing devotion to the sacraments and prayer — an earnest faith. "And thank God," he reminded everyone, showing happy people to the monastery door.

On January 4, 1922, a special Mass and celebration was scheduled. Father Solanus was celebrating twenty-five years in the Capuchin order. He was very new to this parish, but no one would have thought so. A somewhat playful entry in the monastery's chronicle for the day described the outpouring of affection for Father Solanus on the day. "A great multitude of the population of New York" had called to greet Solanus, the logbook noted.[7]

A quarter-century earlier, on that day, a restless twenty-six-year-old had finally found some peace when the brown Franciscan habit had been slipped over his head. With it, he was given the new name Frater Francis Solanus. The weeks prior to this day had tormented his spirit with doubts. He had wanted to leave St. Bonaventure, leave the Capuchins, and leave Detroit!

In the years that followed that long-ago January day in 1897, the first part of his given religious name, "Francis," had almost been forgotten. He was known simply as Frater Solanus and later as Father Solanus. But the brown hooded habit with the white knotted cord seemed to fit him perfectly right from the start. In it, and in his life as a Capuchin friar, he would become more and more comfortable.

After the twenty-fifth year celebration, the friars' house at Queen of Angels returned more or less to normal. The lines of people seeking to talk with Father Solanus grew still longer. But by now, that seemed to be the normal, predictable result of the doorkeeper's remarkable gifts.

Often, Father Solanus could be seen protesting to those whose prayers had been answered. He would insist that such "favors" could be given from God's hands no matter who had enrolled the petitioner in the SMA. Nonetheless, province directors noted that very few claims for healings or answered prayers were originating from other SMA enrollments in other monasteries.

In September of 1922, Father Solanus sat down at an old typewriter and labored over a letter that was unlike any others written during the year. He was outraged at two editorials printed in the *Catholic News* about the Irish-British situation. The gentleness and easygoing docility left Father Solanus when it came to this subject of Irish oppression. He became fiery, as the editors of the *Catholic News* soon discovered. Over this subject and other "social justice" topics, he could become very assertive and impassioned.

In five typed pages, he poured out a tirade against Britain's "Ireland policies." "If Britain is in favor of the said 'Free State' — and she seems to mightily so — then, honest, unselfish lovers of Ireland, and of truth, and of justice, ought to be opposed to it." He referred to "Britain-broken Treaties" and British hypocrisy and stated that "the English government or the people composing it cannot be honestly or unselfishly interested in Ireland."[8] When the *News* rejected the letter, Solanus turned around and mailed it to *The Irish World* in Manhattan, which ran it word for word.

In the late autumn of 1923, Father Benno Aichinger made his scheduled and official visit to the house and parish at 113th and Third Avenue. Father Benno was the minister of the Capuchin province and was known as "Father Provincial."[9]

Father Benno spent some time learning about the progress of pastoral efforts within the parish. It was also his role to inquire after the spiritual and temporal welfare of each friar within the house. He wanted to know about the ministry of each friar and wanted to hear about any problems being experienced.

It's likely that Father Benno talked for a while to the superior of Queen of Angels before he asked him to call in Father Solanus. By this time, rumors that Father Solanus was a "miracle worker" had spread far enough to be heard by the most influential Capuchin ears. Father Benno was concerned about the situation.

It was not Franciscan philosophy to permit any friar to bask in the limelight of excessive popularity. And certainly not as a "mircle man"! But Father Benno knew something of Father Solanus. He had been briefed about his struggles in the seminary and his ordination as a priest with limited faculties. He had heard that Solanus had accepted all things with great grace.

On November 8, 1923, Father Solanus was summoned to talk with Father Provincial. Just as he had heard, Father Benno could see that he had nothing to fear from the attitude of Father Solanus. Father Solanus spoke of the phenomenal occurrences as "favors" from God. It seemed that he was trying to redirect credit for these "favors" in the proper direction.

These "favors" were being granted through the grace of the Seraphic Mass Association, Solanus explained. He also told Father Benno that he simply talked with people, enrolled them in the SMA, and then prayed for their intentions.

Father Benno studied the honest blue eyes, the straight features of Solanus. The face was still very youthful, he noticed. Finally, Father Benno told Father Solanus to begin to separately record all the prayer requests of those who came to see him. If and when prayers were answered, Father Benno added, Father Solanus was to go back and make note of that "favor" near the original entry. Solanus bowed his head in obedience. He promised that he would do all that the Capuchin provincial had ordered.

When Solanus left Father Benno, he went to look around the house for a notebook he might use. He knew very well that there would be a need for it very quickly. People would come to see him on the following day. Finally, he came across a twelve-by-ten ledger-style notebook with heavy covers. It would do nicely, Solanus told himself. He sat down and thought for a moment about a title.[10]

"Notes about Special Cases." Solanus penned that at the top of his first page and then proceeded to make a short notation about this notebook's newly ordained purpose. "Nov. 8th, 1923," Father Solanus wrote. "Today Visitation closed. Father Provincial wishes notes to be made of special favors reported as through the Seraphic Mass Association."

The closed "Visitation" referred to the fact that for that day, the monastery welcomed no visitors and did none of its usual business because of the visit of the provincial. Father Solanus had no people to meet and talk with at his front office desk. The whole day was given over to meeting with the provincial and hearing his pastoral advice. Later, Father Benno made his good-byes and headed for the next Capuchin stop. Within a short time, Solanus had occasion to pick up his pen and his notebook about "Special Cases." He made the first entry.

86

"This P.M. Marg. Quinn — who enrolled her neighbor Mr. Maughan against drink and consequent anger on October 26, as also her sister, E. Remy of Philadelphia against severe inflammatory rheumatism, reports wonderful improvement in former and [reception of] letter this A.M. from [her] sister [writing]: 'Thank God and the good prayer society, I'm feeling fine.' "

Underneath his first entry Solanus jotted "Thanks be to God!"[11] From November 8 to December 9, 1923, a wide variety of intentions were jotted on the first page of the notebook. The needs for prayer represented a good cross-section of human aspirations and complaints.

One woman from Connecticut came to ask Father Solanus to pray for a religious vocation for her son. Another mother arrived in tears because her sixteen-year-old daughter had disappeared. A woman came and enrolled her brother who had had a serious drinking problem for five years. A couple who had been mugged showed up only to receive tender first aid and a prayer for healing from the doorkeeper. A petitioner asked prayers to alleviate a nervous condition while another asked prayers to relieve a condition which had made her blind in one eye.[12]

Squeezed into the margin near the entry about the drinking brother, another "Thanks be to God" appeared. It was dated December 14, five days after the original entry was made. The woman had come to report that her brother had suddenly stopped drinking and that she was "hopeful."

As Christmas of 1923 came closer, the briefly worded, abbreviated notations on needs continued to be recorded. More entries carried happy follow-up reports.

A woman dying of pneumonia recovered. She'd been given only a few hours to live. Another woman came back to tell Father Solanus that her life-threatening heart condition had cleared up. A woman who had lost her memory eight years earlier regained it, her husband came to tell Father Solanus. A New Jersey man hospitalized in an asylum was healed and reported back to work within four months, his family told Solanus.[13]

Men, women, and children, believers and nonbelievers alike — all seemed to be the beneficiaries of Solanus's enrollment in the SMA. There was no rhyme or rhythm to the remarkable reports of favors. "God is good!" "Thank God!" Solanus repeatedly told dumbfounded people who had returned to Queen of Angels to tell of their blessings. There is no mystery to it, he insisted.

It's true that some sick people certainly improved in a way that may have occurred in the normal course of events. But in other cases, the turnaround seemed totally unexplainable from a medical perspective.

In a letter written to Father Provincial in January of 1924, Father Solanus mentioned the great financial blessings which the SMA was bringing to the missions. "Fr. Guardian just told me that the cash received this month already is $1002.00," he wrote. "Thanks be to God! the report of favors as through this source continue."[14]

In February of 1924, a man named Patrick McCue was enrolled in the Seraphic Mass Association by a friend. McCue, a motorman, was in Belleview Hospital, suffering from diabetes and a gangrenous toe. Doctors told him that it was likely that his leg would have to be amputated. McCue's condition took a sudden and complete turn for the better, however, after the SMA enrollment. Surgery was called off; the infection disappeared on its own. By the end of March, Patrick McCue was back at work.[15]

Gradually, people came from increasingly distant locations to ask for counsel and prayers from Father Solanus. This meant that word of the special ministry was being spread farther afield by those who had already had contact with him.

Whatever the superiors of Father Solanus were waiting to see was very soon visible to them. On July 30, he was told that they had decided to move him once again. This time, the move was to be out of New York and back to Detroit. St. Bonaventure's, after all, was headquarters for the order. It was large and had no parish attached.

If the ministry of Father Solanus was going to continue to

attract crowds of people daily, perhaps it could be better handled in Detroit. Between November 8, 1923, and July 28, 1924, Solanus had made ninety-six entries about cases in his notebook. Later, it was seen that forty-one of them carried added notations indicating that prayers had been answered.[16]

Within two days, Father Solanus had dutifully and punctually reported at St. Bonaventure's — by his August 1 deadline.[17] No farewell banquets had been arranged and there'd been little time to wrap up any unfinished commitments to people or projects at Our Lady, Queen of Angels Parish. Solanus knew he would be leaving a part of his heart in New York at Sacred Heart, at Our Lady of Sorrows, and at Queen of Angels.

Years later, Solanus wrote to his brother Jim of his New York leave-taking. "While I never long to go back to any old place from which Divine Providence has seen good to remove me, yet I must acknowledge that I have a natural inclination that way — like the Israelites in the desert naturally yearning (many of them) to go back to Egypt."[18]

With some twinges of that longing inside of him, Father Solanus found himself making his way to his assigned room on a hot day in Detroit. He needed to unpack. That may have taken even less time than it had when he'd arrived at St. Bonaventure's the first time.

That arrival, in 1896, had been a snowy, stormy Christmas Eve. On this warm August day in 1924, Solanus could only look back at that day of entrance and the stinging December cold and wonder. He was astonished — prayerfully astonished — at the ministry into which the Lord had been leading him right from the beginning.

CHAPTER SEVEN

Back at St. Bonaventure's (1924-1935)

By 1924, Detroit was rapidly becoming "the Motor City," the automobile center of the world. In 1913, Henry Ford had already settled on an assembly-line approach that was to revolutionize automobile production. In the decade following, the future looked bright and exciting for the city. Even the Capuchin monastery on Mt. Elliott Avenue on the city's east side was becoming comfortable with a few twentieth-century comforts.

In 1897, the year before Father Solanus had moved on to study in Milwaukee, the friars had decided to put in electric lights. The chapel and all the rooms of St. Bonaventure had warmed them with the glow of modern lighting. Ten years later, in 1907, a hot-water heating system was installed to heat the chapel when the old system failed. Friars, after all, spent hours in prayer, sitting or kneeling in an otherwise chilly chapel. In 1909, the first telephone was installed and the Capuchins then had a link to the outside world.[1]

During a short talk with the superior of the house, Father Solanus discovered that he would again be a sort of human link to that outside world. His official assignment was to be assistant porter, helping out the friary porter, Brother Francis Spruck. Unofficially, it was expected that his role of counseling and praying with people would continue. It was thought that Brother Francis needed help, since he was also the tailor for the province. Brother Francis had to cut and sew the habits for men all over the province. To facilitate his dual role, Brother Francis had been given two rooms near the friary's main entrance. The tailor shop was on the right side of the door with a porter's office on the other.

By the early autumn of 1924, however, Brother Francis and Father Solanus both saw that the visitor lines there at St. Bonaventure were getting longer as the days went by. Most of the visitors, it seemed, wanted to meet or talk with Father Solanus.

The guardian, Father Innocent Ferstler, and others who heard about the work Father Solanus had done in New York were not surprised by the lines. And Solanus Casey certainly could not have been surprised. He had become very familiar with the powerful needs of spirit and body among all God's people. Those needs were just as common in Detroit as in Manhattan and Yonkers.

Brother Francis Spruck, however, was at first shocked and later distressed by the long lines of petitioners winding their way around the friary's front hall. His job as main porter had once been a manageable one. Now that he had an "assistant," the "routine" portering tasks were getting more and more demanding. There was a crowd in the place every day! His "assistant" was creating more work for him!

Neither could Francis understand why Solanus spent so much time talking with each person. As the doorbell began to ring more and more frequently, Brother Francis found himself having to leave his tailoring table to answer it. Father Solanus, he noticed, was almost always too preoccupied in a conversation to answer the door. Visitors told Brother Francis that they wanted to see Solanus, that they had heard that his prayers were so often answered.

Francis nodded politely. Yet, it seemed to Francis that a scheduled limit of time spent with each person would be more efficient. It was a suggestion that Father Solanus listened to very attentively but never seemed to act upon. Instead, chairs were set up along the walls. Waiting to see Father Solanus became a bit less tiring but no less time-consuming.

In one way, the front-door phenomenon surrounding Father Solanus was more disruptive for St. Bonaventure's than it had been in the parishes where he'd been assigned. At St. Bonaventure, the Capuchins had no parish attached to the monastery. It had been planned that way. When it was founded in 1883, restrictions had been imposed on the scheduling of High Masses and sermons by the archdiocese.[2]

That had been done to prevent St. Bonaventure's from drawing people away from parishes. The Capuchins could not have been happier about the "restraints." At this monastery, they wanted the chance for quiet prayer, and the methodical, monastic way of life provided it.

Though Brother Francis had little sympathy for him, Solanus Casey struggled to blend his day at the porter's desk with the routine prayer life in the monastery. The community rose for the day at 4:45 A.M. Father Solanus was often up earlier than that, praying in the chapel. Following night prayer, the other Capuchins were in bed by 9:30 P.M. Frequently, the assistant porter was still talking at that hour to a visitor or two at his desk at the front entrance. It was a wearying pace for anyone, and by now Solanus Casey was in his fifties.

Frequently, Brother Francis would scold Solanus in front of waiting people, calling him simply "Solanus!" when he was irritated. Francis would then announce that people could also come to him for enrollment in the Seraphic Mass Association. Making no retort, Father Solanus would meekly nod his head and agree. No one left his seat, however. People preferred to wait for Father Solanus, even if it took twice as long.[3] And it frequently did.

"I have plenty to keep myself busy for at least eighteen hours a day," he wrote many years later to his sister Margaret.[4] But, by then, the eighteen-hour workday had been part of his life for dozens of years.

In New York, Solanus had made many friends. In Detroit, the same sort of enduring relationships began to develop very soon after Solanus arrived. In January of 1925, Solanus met Earl Eagen, a thirty-nine-year-old husband and father from Port Huron, Michigan. Eagen was in pain and in a state of hopelessness with stomach cancer. The man was in such a low state that Solanus later said that he had judged him to be seventy-five years old or older. Eagen told the porter that he didn't know who would care for his children.

Following a pattern that had begun in New York, Father Solanus asked Earl Eagen and his wife if he could enroll them in the Seraphic Mass Association. The Eagens readily agreed to it and promised to donate money for a "perpetual enrollment" as soon as they could afford it.

Eight days later, a rejuvenated Earl Eagen and his wife drove the sixty miles to Detroit on a Sunday morning. Eagen told Father Solanus that the stomach pains were gone and that he felt totally well. He was not at all sure, he told the priest, that he would even bother to have the X rays done which could confirm the disappearance of the cancer. Solanus, smiling with delight, agreed that the money might be better spent for the SMA. A long friendship with the Eagen family began right then and there.[5]

On February 4, 1925, a couple from a Detroit suburb brought their nine-year-old son to see Father Solanus. The boy, John Slyker, had very serious vision problems which were puzzling the eye specialists who had seen him. John was experiencing double vision in one eye and had no vision in the other. On the way home from St. Bonaventure, after Father Solanus had blessed him and enrolled him in the SMA, John began to read street signs. An "unexplainable" but immediate improvement of his vision had begun.[6]

As the 1920s had proceeded, signs of economic troubles ahead began to surface in Detroit. A sluggishness in the automobile industry became apparent. Production slowdowns forced the major companies to cut working hours for most of their employees. Many of the Detroiters whom Solanus knew grew worried.

In March of 1925, John McKenna, a Chevrolet employee, came to talk with Solanus. He told his Capuchin friend how worried he was about his ability to support his wife and children. Due to the economic slump, hours at Chevrolet had been reduced to a handful of hours of work per day. Suddenly, McKenna suggested to Father Solanus that the whole company — Chevrolet — be enrolled in the Seraphic Mass Association.

Solanus considered the unusual request for just a moment. He had enrolled invididuals in the SMA. He had enrolled families, too. But he had never thought of enrolling a body of people, such as an entire company. Could a company benefit from the graces ensuing from offered Mass intentions and Capuchin prayers? Father Solanus didn't really see why such an unusual enrollment couldn't be made. He winked at McKenna and reached for his pen. The wink said simply that God can answer prayer in any way he wishes.

On that same day, John McKenna later heard, Chevrolet had received a very large order for automobiles. Soon after, an order for forty-five thousand cars was placed, and Chevrolet employees were ordered back to work, and even on overtime at that. As soon as he heard that news, an overjoyed McKenna visited Father Solanus to give him the good news.[7]

There was no question about the fact that this unique ministry and his demanding schedule set him apart from other friars. Clearly, the service Father Solanus was involved in was following no other Capuchin patterns.

Solanus, for instance, was almost always late for meals. He was reluctant to cut off people who had come to seek his help just because his dinner or supper or breakfast was about to be served. "I think he just about ate the one main meal," said a fellow friar.[8] Brother Francis, who had trouble understanding the Solanus approach, would frequently enter the refectory explaining that Father Solanus was "still talking, still talking."

Francis seemed to believe that Solanus was too "loose" in the way he dealt with visitors. More control over the situation through tighter scheduling of personal conferences, he believed, would save the monastery and Solanus much inconvenience.

Some mannerisms and traits in Father Solanus also prompted teasing from other friars at St. Bonaventure. But Solanus Casey wasn't unfamiliar with that sort of thing. He had been raised in a family of sixteen children. He shrugged off the jokes about his high-pitched wispy voice. "Nobody understands you; open your mouth!" he was told. "God understands me," he would comment.[9]

Solanus, they noticed, also had an unusual eating habit which looked, at first glance, as a very strange and unpalatable habit. In the morning, at breakfast, he would pour everything he was consuming into one bowl with his cereal. Coffee and orange juice would slosh around in the bowl with cold or hot cereal. It's likely that it was a sort of self-imposed mortification, but some of his brother Capuchins teased him continually about it. When somewhat sharper remarks were made about his violin-playing, Solanus seemed to turn a deaf ear to them. It was a matter of give and take. He took the wisecracks and gave his concerts anyway.

With the time he had, Father Solanus did make efforts to be as fully involved as possible in community life. He enjoyed people, and when the friars met at recreation time, Solanus liked to participate. On Sunday evenings, he would come into the refectory and pour himself a glass of wine from the gallon jug by holding it over his shoulder. He was clearly ready to mix with others and enjoy himself. He had a natural knack for spinning tales about Ireland, his childhood, or youth. Playing billiards or pool was a favorite game and he was considered a tough opponent, until his call bell or a phone call would interrupt his game. Then, his brother Capuchins recalled, he would hang up his pool cue and head for his porter's desk. He knew he wouldn't be back too quickly.[10]

The visitors continued to come, day after day, month after

month. The front door of the monastery had always been locked in the past. Now, it was open all the time. Solanus had hung a sign outside which said "Walk in." It eliminated the prospect of a doorbell ringing constantly. Sitting at his desk, Father Solanus continued to enroll hundreds of people in the Seraphic Mass Association. As the seasons moved on by the Capuchin monastery on Mt. Elliott Avenue, the pattern did not change much. And the "favors" being reported didn't stop.

On January 20, 1927, thirty-year-old Anna Schram was taken from her Detroit home to the hospital for surgery. One month after an operation for gallstones, doctors told her that she had developed an abscess of the liver. They admitted that they did not know of any patient who had survived such an operation. Anna's sister phoned Father Solanus at St. Bonaventure and had Anna enrolled. Less than one month after Father Solanus had enrolled the young woman in the SMA, her sister told Solanus that Anna was already home and was recovering.[11]

Visitors were also recovering from illnesses and complaints following the Wednesday afternoon healing service. It was a service held each week at 3:00 P.M. in the chapel. For years, the Capuchins had been offering a blessing called the "St. Maurus Blessing of the Sick." The blessing had a Benedictine history and had come from a sixth-century monk named Maurus who had a gift of healing.

When Father Solanus moved to St. Bonaventure's, the prayer service grew in popularity. But it was a struggle for Solanus himself to get there on time. Right up until the clock struck three, Father Solanus would be at his desk, meeting with someone. Finally, Brother Francis stood directly in front of Solanus and his visitor, tapping his foot and whispering sharply, "Casey!" Then Father Solanus would quietly apologize that he had to leave. The two, Francis and Solanus, would walk through a hallway which connected the friary to the chapel. Disappointed people waiting to see and talk with Father Solanus either followed him to church to attend the service or waited for his return.[12] At dinner later in the day, Francis frequently scolded Solanus for all of his "idle words."[13]

Following a short *ferverino* or talk at the healing service, Father Solanus would bless those attending with a relic of the true cross. He always wore the same red stole and used a relic of the true cross which he had obtained. Solanus was not always assigned to lead the service, but when he was scheduled for it, people arrived early and sat at the front of the chapel.

His weak voice made him hard to hear. Those who came wanted to hear his words. The words almost always touched on trust in God, thanking God, or the virtues of faith and charity. The blessing of St. Maurus was then pronounced for all: "Through the invocation of the most holy name of the Lord may that faith, in which St. Maurus, by employing the words that follow, healed the sick, and in which I, though an unworthy servant, utter the selfsame words, restore your health as you desire. In the name of the most holy and undivided Trinity, and supported by the merits of the most holy Father Benedict, I bid you to rise, stand on your feet, and be cured. In the name of the Father, and of the Son, and of the Holy Ghost. Amen."

Near the end of 1928, Father Maurice came to visit his brother Father Solanus at St. Bonaventure's. Maurice was then sixty-one years old and had been a priest for seventeen years. But Father Maurice was not settled, and Solanus listened, as he listened to so many people, with great attention. Maurice, it seemed, wanted to become a member of the Capuchin order and leave the diocesan priesthood.

Father Solanus knew that his brother had not been happy in his parish ministry in the West, but he couldn't quite understand the reason for it. Nonetheless, he arranged for Maurice to talk to the superiors of the order about becoming a Capuchin. By the end of his visit with his younger brother, Maurice was able to plan that he would be returning to enter the Capuchin novitiate during the following year. He left Detroit happy, but Father Solanus was troubled. On Christmas Eve, his worries about Maurice were overshadowed by other family news. Ellie — as the eldest of the Casey siblings was called — had died in Seattle at the age of sixty-four.

The last year of the 1920s began in a very predictable way,

as far as the Capuchins of St. Bonaventure's were concerned. The weather was cold and wet. And the lines of visitors coming to talk with Father Solanus were filled with people with anxious eyes. There were also phone calls and people at the door in the middle of the night.

"Any time that anyone came to the monastery at night, Father Solanus would answer the bell," remembered Father Herman Buss, whose room was adjacent to Solanus's. "None of the others were inclined to disturb their rest. I would always hear the 'slop-slop' of his sandals."[14]

On January 25, 1929, Father Solanus heard the doorbell again and got up. A Western Union delivery man was holding a telegram addressed to him. After closing the door, he tore the telegram open. His brothers John and Tom had been killed that evening in a car accident near Seattle. John, fifty-nine, and Tom, fifty-four, were both lawyers and had been on their way home after trying a case together. Solanus bit his lip with the pain and made his way to the chapel. Three from his family gone in less than a month!

In the spring and summer, hundreds of people continued to make their way to Mt. Elliott Avenue. Some came over from the new Chrysler plant that had been completed nearly a year earlier, in 1928. The plant was to be the last major automobile plant built within the city limits.[15]

In July, Father Solanus marked the twenty-fifth anniversary of his ordination. Maurice came to help him celebrate the occasion and then prepared to enter the Capuchin novitiate. The order had been receiving so many vocations that a new novitiate building was built. It was completed in Huntington, Indiana. Fathers Solanus and Maurice headed for the small community surrounded by farmlands about twenty-five miles southwest of Fort Wayne.

On September 10, with Father Solanus assisting at the ceremony, Maurice was invested as a Capuchin along with a group of young men. Maurice was to be known in the order as Father Maurice Joachim. Eventually, Maurice was accepted into the order as a Third Order member only. (The Third Order is known today as the Secular Franciscan Order.) The Capuchins were apparently reluctant to permit him to profess vows in the congregation at the "advanced" age of sixty-two. Solanus considered that his brother was finally where he should be. Happy about Maurice's new start, Solanus returned to Detroit.[16]

About six weeks after Father Solanus returned, the world began to fall apart. At least, that was the way it seemed to many Detroiters and to millions of other Americans. On October 29, 1929, the Stock Market crashed. It signaled the beginning of a financial collapse which had no historical parallel. Alfred E. Smith, the Catholic New Yorker who'd run for president of the United States as a Democrat the year before, said later that the Great Depression which followed was equivalent to war.[17] People in Detroit believed that they were on the front line of that war.

The disaster probably hit Detroit harder than any other American city. Motor vehicle production dropped from 5.3 million annually in 1929 to 1.3 million by 1932. Detroit had become the most important industrial city in the country by 1930.[18]

It wasn't long before there were even more people lined up at the monastery doors on Mt. Elliott Avenue. But this time, many of them needed something besides prayers and a willing listener. They needed food.

The Capuchins quickly increased the amount of food available for the hungry. In fact, it had always been a practice at the monastery to feed the needy who came to the door. Before the Great Depression really began, about one hundred people came each day for some coffee, soup, and a slice or two of bread. Even this had become too much for the porters Solanus and Francis to handle.[19]

After the Stock Market Crash, Father Capistran Claude, the superior of the monastery, immediately asked the Third Order of St. Francis to help. The Third Order was a group of lay people linked with Franciscans through the pledge to observe certain religious practices and a Francisican spirit. Father Herman Buss, who directed the Third Order, quickly mobilized the group. On November 2, three days after the

Crash, the doors of a soup kitchen were opened for the first time by the Third Order.

At first, only coffee and rolls were available to the hungry. Within a few weeks, members of the Third Order had begun to make a hearty soup which they served at noon. Because of very limited kitchen facilities, they were forced to prepare each day's meal the day before. In the dining room of their hall, rough planks were set up over sawhorses for tables. The hungry were typically men. They began to pour in each day.[20] As the Depression cast more and more people into need, the Capuchin soup kitchen was feeding between fifteen hundred and three thousand people each day.

Father Solanus followed the efforts of the soup kitchen from his desk. At first, he could not become actively involved in the feeding ministry, but his heart was there. When Solanus met people of financial means or influence, he urged them to contribute toward the soup kitchen. Around Christmas time, he met an Irishman named Ray McDonough, who came to help at the soup kitchen after his employer sent him to get involved. With the blessing of the Capuchins and with forty-two dollars, McDonough went over to St. Vincent de Paul Orphanage and bought a potato peeler.[21]

The new decade, the thirties, opened with a heaviness that few Americans could even describe. The crowds in the waiting room at St. Bonaventure grew larger and larger. Many were men who had lost heart after weeks of joblessness and no means of feeding their families. As the months went by, these men were facing foreclosures on homes or evictions from apartments.

Families were being torn apart, and people correctly suspected that the misery would get worse before it got better. The men at the friary shook their heads in disbelief when it was reported that Henry Ford was calling the Depression "a wholesome thing in general."[22] He mandated that all of his workmen dig vegetable gardens in their backyards or on Ford property or be fired.[23]

As a result of this sort of attitude, many came to St. Bonaventure's sensing that their unemployment and their poverty were somehow their own fault. Father Solanus disagreed and shared his vision of how God loved them and would watch over them. He also shared the food reserves of the friary pantry until some of his fellow Capuchins complained.

Father Solanus made it his business to make the needs of the kitchen known to the more influential Detroiters he was meeting. Tom Bresnahan, the mayor of River Rouge, a Detroit suburb, began to send help. Later on, Frank Murphy, Detroit's mayor, donated a prize bull he'd won in a raffle.[24]

Finding enough food to feed as many as three thousand people each day was difficult for the Capuchins. And it was impossible to predict on a daily basis just how many people would be lining up to eat. An excess of even fifty could run the kitchen out of soup and bread and leave hungry people standing with empty plates. All of the Capuchins agonized when it seemed that there might be a shortage.

Father Herman Buss remembered many anxious moments in the kitchen. But one day something happened that he would never forget. He had absolutely no bread to feed a crowd of people already waiting in line. Thinking perhaps that Father Solanus could phone one of his more affluent friends, Father Herman went over to the monastery and told Solanus of the crisis.

"I said, 'Father Solanus, we have no more bread and two or three hundred men are waiting for something to eat.' He went over to the hall and told the men who were waiting in line, 'Just wait and God will provide.' Father Solanus said an 'Our Father' after inviting the men to join him in the prayer. We just turned around and opened the front door to go out, and there was a bakery man coming with a big basket full of food. He had his whole truck full of stuff, and he proceeded to unload it. When the men saw this they started to cry and tears were running down their cheeks. Father Solanus, in his simple way, said, 'See, God provides. Nobody will starve as long as you put your confidence in God, in Divine Providence.' "[25]

In 1931 and 1932, the Capuchins were also beginning to contact Detroit bakeries to ask for donations of day-old bread. And butchers, hearing about the soup kitchen, began to give meat bones for the stockpots. The community as a whole was doing what it could to help its own, to extend a helping hand to those in need. By early 1933, when Franklin Roosevelt was just beginning his first term as president, an estimated twelve million Americans were out of work.[26]

There was little or no money for doctor bills, and illness became even more frightening.

In 1934, the Houlihans' newborn son was exposed to whooping cough. When the tiny baby began to cough, the parents took him to the doctor who gave him a shot. But the coughing continued.

"We took him at once to Father Solanus," Mrs. Houlihan recalled. "As we entered the office, Father Solanus was speaking to someone else — but he looked up at us as we waited our turn. Father Solanus heard our baby son cough and choke up. Father Solanus left his desk and came right over to us and asked what was the trouble with our small baby. Father Solanus blessed the baby and told us not to worry, that our son would be alright."

The baby did recover, although the Houlihans' doctor, a Catholic, frankly admitted that he had expected the child to die. "The doctor told us that we were very fortunate to keep our son."[27]

The largest ethnic group in the city of Detroit was Canadian. With William Tremblay, who often acted as a driver, Solanus occasionally went out to those who were too sick to come to St. Bonaventure. Tremblay remembered a visit to a dying woman, Mrs. Eva Dugall, in Windsor. The woman had tuberculosis and had been on the verge of dying for months, Tremblay said. Anxiety concerning the welfare of her small children kept her alive.

"Father went inside and I went along too. When he came in, the first thing this lady said was, 'Oh, you look just like Jesus Christ Himself.' Everybody in the room began to cry. 'Well, I'm taking His place,' he said. 'I was sent here by Him. I

102

came because the Lord has a crown waiting for you. Why don't you resign yourself to go to Heaven and forget about your children? The Lord has a lot of good mothers, especially the Blessed Virgin, and she will take care of your children.' "

The woman became peaceful, Tremblay said. Everyone began to pray after Father Solanus suggested they say a decade of the Rosary. Then Solanus and his driver left. At 11:00 P.M. that evening, Tremblay discovered, the woman died, leaving her pain behind.[28]

Confidence in God. If any phrase summed up the vision of life of this Capuchin, that was it. But Solanus was not under the impression that confidence in God meant inaction on the part of those in need. He was country-bred. When there was something he could do, he rolled up his sleeves, figuratively — and literally, too.

One of the burdens of maintaining an adequate food supply was a blessing in the eyes of Father Solanus. It was necessary to go out to area farms and pick fruit or vegetables. Solanus loved to go out in a truck with Ray McDonough, who had become the director of the Capuchin soup kitchen. McDonough would drive and Father Solanus would feast his eyes on fields and farms. Somewhere along the trip, the two would say a Rosary for the poor and for the success of their venture.

"Father Solanus accompanied Ray Garland with a truck on a begging trip near Ruth [Michigan]," the chronicle of St. Bonaventure reported on October 25, 1934. "They returned with a load of apples, potatoes, and other vegetables at 2 a.m." Another note entered a month later reported Solanus out again in the Ruth area with Brother Paschal collecting fifty bushels of potatoes, thirty bags of beans, and other foodstuffs.[29]

The deepening of the Great Depression throughout the 1930s stretched reserves to the limits. And the ministry of Father Solanus must have also been taxed. As the expectations of others increased, so did his prayer life. He could not help thinking of the people who came to see him and of their problems. Fatigue and the tediousness of his routine were often overwhelming, he admitted later. By nature, he was not a work-

103

aholic. As a boy and later in life, he enjoyed leisure very much, but it was rapidly disappearing from his life.

Detroit people began to talk of a sort of "knowledge" in Solanus. He seemed to have an inner sense or prophetic sense about the outcome of many events. Father Solanus had always told troubled visitors to pray with faith. But his assurance about events often seemed to go beyond "believing" to become "knowing."

In 1933, according to Mrs. Mary Therese McHugh, her two-year-old daughter became very ill and developed a 104-degree fever. The doctor told Mrs. McHugh that it was a life-threatening situation, but soon the child's fever went even higher. There seemed to be little chance to save her life. Mrs. McHugh's pastor suggested that she call Father Solanus at St. Bonaventure's. Solanus told her to bring the child over to him immediately.

Mrs. McHugh wrapped up the child and drove over to the monastery. Father Solanus took the little girl into his own arms and prayed silently for a few moments. Then, he returned the child to her mother and told her to come back with the child on Saturday — three days later.

"I told him that the doctors did not expect her to live until Saturday," Mrs. McHugh said later.

"Just do as I wish. Bring her to me; she'll be ready," Father Solanus responded.

For Father Solanus, there was no question about the outcome for this child. He seemed to be convinced that she would not only recover but would be well enough to leave the house within three days.

That night, as Mrs. McHugh recalled years later, her little girl's fever broke and she began to recover. In the morning, little Marianne woke up and began to ask for something to eat. The McHughs' doctor viewed the child's recovery as "a miracle." It was a miracle that Father Solanus could apparently see coming.[30]

Many of the miracles that seemed to touch Father Solanus most personally had to do with conversions — healings of the heart and of the spirit. Some times such feelings changed the direction of the person's life dramatically . . . and humorously. Solanus reported on one such conversion to his good friend William Tremblay years later.

Early one morning during these early 1930s, around four o'clock, Solanus got up to answer the doorbell at the front entrance. He was one of the monstery porters, after all. A man who'd obviously been drinking stood waiting for him on the step.

"Where's that guy Solanus?" the man wanted to know, slurring his words a bit.

"Well, he's here. What do you want with him?" Solanus answered.

"I came here to kill him," the man replied.

"Well," Solanus said, "that's something that should be discussed."

The porter then invited this would-be murderer into the monastery and sat him down on the other side of his desk. In a few moments, the man spilled out the reasons for his desire to kill a priest he'd never met. He was a Communist, he told Father Solanus, but his mother was a devoted Catholic and was a friend of this Father Solanus. She cried all the time about her son's Communist views and his abandonment of the Church. The man was tired of her interference and even more tired of hearing about Solanus.

Solanus listened patiently. He nodded appreciatively and even smiled a bit. When the fellow was all talked out and sobered just a bit, Father Solanus began to talk. He talked about the Church, about God's mercy, and about the godlessness of Communism. By the time Father Solanus was finished, the man's heart was completely changed. He wanted to go to confession. Besides the fact that he was not permitted to hear anyone's confession, Father Solanus wanted the man to receive the blessings of Penance when he was completely sober. Father Solanus told him that he should come back later in the light of day to do that. When the man left, Solanus shut off the lights and headed for the chapel. The monastery day started at 4:45 A.M., anyway.[31]

CHAPTER EIGHT

Longer Lines and Longer Hours (1935-1945)

On May 16, 1935, the chronicler at St. Bonaventure Monastery had a rather strange incident to record about the assistant porter, Father Solanus Casey. He wrote: "Father Solanus to his great joy recovered his Mass Association Record book. He had misplaced it a few days ago but could not recall where he had put it. He went to the Post Office and found it there." The chronicler goes on to explain the probable sequence of events: Father Solanus had placed his record book with a bundle of letters he had just picked up at the post office. On the way out, without thinking he dropped the bundle of mail — along with his Seraphic Mass Association ledger — in a mailbox. Postal employees, later discovering the letters and ledger, contacted a grateful Father Solanus.[1]

Since he had come to Detroit to the Capuchin provincialate eleven years earlier, Solanus Casey had been living at such a pace! It would have finished many sixty-four-year-old men. As a result, there was little time and little mental energy left to sort things, let alone information, into the proper "incoming" and "outgoing" categories. Life was hectic, and only the peace of prayer and the Blessed Sacrament in the chapel seemed to make it tolerable.

Throughout the summer of 1935, Solanus was also serving on weekend "help-outs" at Detroit parishes. Generally, it meant saying several Masses and then returning to the friary. He was at the friary on the day Brother André Bessette of Montreal stopped to visit him. Brother André, a French Canadian Holy Cross brother, was then ninety. Like Solanus, he had also been a porter and had become famous in Canada. Thousands claimed healings through his prayers and special devotion to St. Joseph.

When they met, Brother André asked Father Solanus for his blessing. It was given. Father Solanus in turn asked for and received the aged brother's blessing.[2] Then the two parted. It was a brief meeting, for Father Solanus spoke no French and Brother André did not speak English. But perhaps the calling of God's blessing upon each other said everything they needed to say to each other.

On November 25, Solanus turned sixty-five. This birthday may not have seemed any different from other birthdays. There was no thought of his retirement — either in his mind or in the minds of his superiors at St. Bonaventure's Monastery. The beard was totally gray now and there was very little hair on the top of his head. His oldest brother, Jim, the oldest surviving sibling, had reached his seventieth birthday.

It was a considerable consolation for Solanus that Jim and his other brothers and sisters were doing well and were relatively healthy. The Casey clan was prospering. A good healthy crop of fourth-generation Caseys — grandchildren of his brothers and sisters — was being born and growing up, mostly in the Far West.

The parishes and friends he'd come to know in New York were fondly recalled, but Solanus seemed to be in the right place at St. Bonaventure's. Detroit was sure of it. In one of the most difficult eras of its history, during these years of the Great Depression, Father Solanus had become something of a local celebrity.

The reputation of Father Solanus had its predictable result as the 1930s moved along. More and more people came to St. Bonaventure's to see him. The reasons for their visits were no different than the visits of hundreds who had come before: failing eyesight, terminal diseases, marital difficulties, dying children, joblessness, anxiety, depression, the desire for a spiritual conversion of a husband, wife, brother, son. Though the names and faces were difficult, the stories must have seemed very familiar to Father Solanus month after month, year after year.

Many doctors in the Motor City were also hearing of the priest who seemed to have a connection with miraculous healings. After Father Solanus prayed for sick individuals, some went back to their physicians later. More than one doctor could offer no explanation for a sudden cessation of a disease or for the apparent overnight healing of bones or injured tissue or muscles. One of the Capuchin guardians, Father Marion Roessler, recalled a hospital's offer of records to substantiate "healing" claims. "I recall on one occasion that we received word from a Catholic hospital in Detroit, that their authorities would willingly furnish the medical history and x-ray plates of some cases which were suddenly cured after the patients had received the assurance of Father Solanus' prayers, his blessing, and/or his enrolling them in the Seraphic Mass Association. However, I no longer remember the name of that hospital."[3]

Father Marion Roessler was more clear about the details of a healing he himself saw during these years. "It was the cure of a crippled child who had not walked in years," Father Marion reported later. "She was held in the lap of an adult, sitting at some distance from Father Solanus' desk. Father Solanus enrolled the child in the Seraphic Mass Association, and blessed her. Then he told her to walk over to him. She immediately got to her feet and walked, going straight to his desk. The youngsters' parents were amost hysterical with joy."[4] When healings occurred instantly, tears would well up in the blue eyes of Solanus. Witnessing the goodness of God understandably moved him.

Father Solanus may have placed his greatest trust in God as healer, but he never rejected the need for medical doctors. He frequently suggested that people go to doctors to identify ailments or to seek continuing treatment for a health problem. And yet, he also advised that doctors would not be helpful in certain cases or that they simply were not needed. This sort of counsel proved controversial even though there never was an example of damaging advice from Solanus with respect to medical care.[5]

The foreknowledge that the porter seemed to have was as awesome as the gift of healing working through him. And reports of this ability to foresee events were circulating more frequently in Detroit in the thirties. "God will take care of it for you," he told hundreds of people who eventually saw healings or resolved problems. Solanus, it seems, could see when one patient would improve and when another would be dying. In 1935, this gift of prophecy was demonstrated in a visit one day to two patients at St. Joseph Mercy Hospital.

Father Solanus had been phoned and asked to visit a Sister Mary Joseph. She was desperately ill with a severe streptococcus infection on the right side of her throat. Her fever had risen to 105 degrees and her neck had gone rigid. She was slipping into a coma while suffering choking spells. Antibiotics such as penicillin and Terramycin (a brand name for oxytetracycline) were not yet in use. The doctors had told the nun who was the hospital supervisor that they feared the worst for Sister Mary Joseph.

When Father Solanus arrived, he went to the sick nun's bedside and began to read about Christ's Passion in the Gospels. Though Sister Mary Joseph had been coughing when he began, the choking spell soon passed. Solanus also blessed her with the relic of the true cross which he used during Wednesday healing services. After two hours of reading and prayer, he told the nuns assembled around Sister Mary Joseph's hospital bed that she would recover and join them soon.

On the way out of the hospital, however, a man stopped Father Solanus in the hallway. His wife had just had minor surgery, he told the priest. Then he asked the Capuchin if he would stop at her room for a moment just to bless her. Father Solanus did so. But as he left the woman's room, the priest put his hand on the husband's arm and told him that his wife would soon die.

Solanus gently asked the shocked man to give his wife back to her Creator. Then Solanus quietly turned and headed for a car with the hospital chauffeur who was to drive him back to St. Bonaventure. Later, the driver learned that the man's wife had died a short time after they had walked out of the hospital.[6]

In 1936, Father Solanus was involved in the reconciliation of a husband and wife when a bitter separation and divorce seemed inevitable. William Tremblay remembered the situation because the unnamed couple were friends. The husband had confessed to him one day that he'd been having an affair but wanted to break it off. The "other woman," however, threatened to expose his sins to his wife if he abandoned the illicit relationship. Tremblay told his friend to tell his wife about it and then took the two to see his other friend Solanus. Father Solanus had been briefed about the situation before the three arrived.

After Tremblay walked in with the couple and introduced them to Father Solanus, he turned around to leave them with him. "Oh, no," Father Solanus told Tremblay, "you stay right here. You went through all that trouble and you might have a good idea." And so, Tremblay, feeling fairly embarrassed, stayed for the confrontation.

"They were both crying and angry, especially her," Tremblay reported. "She didn't even want to look at him. So Father Solanus told him to tell his story. 'I don't want you to leave anything out. Say everything.'" When the husband began to tell the whole story, his wife wept harder and harder until it was all over.

Then, according to Tremblay, Solanus turned to the wife and urged her to forgive her husband, saying, "Well, that isn't so bad, the man is repentant. The Lord forgave Mary Magdalene, and you have three lovely children outside waiting for the father and mother to get together again." Solanus urged the woman to get up, kiss her husband, and forgive him. She did, and according to Tremblay, their marriage not only survived, it prospered.[7]

In 1936 or 1937, a Detroit woman, Agnes Juergens, developed a terrible pain in her right wrist. Her family physician referred her to a bone specialist. X-ray films revealed a large, web-structured tumor spreading throughout the bones. Trying to remove the tumor, the authorities maintained, would cause the tumor to spread. They advised the patient, a wife and mother, that they would have to amputate her arm at the elbow.

"When the doctor said that they would have to amputate, we went to see Father Solanus," Mrs. Juergens said more than twenty years later. "Father Solanus took my hand, held the wrist, and his eyes were closed. He was praying like he saw a vision or something. When he opened his eyes, he said, 'No, we're not going to let them amputate.' I could just feel that he was seeing something like a vision, that he could see that I would not have to have that operation. After that was when the change began."

"The change" was a halt to the tumor growth. Doctors later verified it and three months of treatments apparently dissolved the tumor. "They did not have to amputate," Mrs Juergens said. "They were so amazed that my arm was saved."[8]

Healings reported through Father Solanus touched bodies, spirits, relationships, and sometimes all three.

In 1936, a suburban Detroit resident named Mrs. Martin Wachinger began to take a woman to the Wednesday prayer services at which Father Solanus almost always served as leader. The woman Mrs. Wachinger took with her was a relative who suffered terrible trauma as a result of brain surgery.

111

During the surgery, a physician told Mrs. Wachinger, an optical nerve had been severed. The woman was rendered blind, mentally incompetent, and wasn't expected to survive long.

After about six months of attendance at the Wednesday services, Mrs. Wachinger noticed that the woman's general health seemed to improve. Finally, eyesight returned to one eye and then to the other. Later still, she began to speak and recover mental faculties. Four years later, the woman whom doctors had given up on had recovered so much that she enrolled in a secretarial course. After obtaining a job, the woman got married and kept her own house. Throughout it all, she lived in good health and in happiness once seen as "impossible."[9]

In October of 1936, Father Solanus learned that his younger brother Leo had died in Seattle. Leo was only fifty-eight. With the death of Leo, three of his nine brothers were gone. Solanus always longed to be closer to his family, but on certain occasions the desire sometimes grew keener. Despite the long days, there was still time for Solanus to write to his brothers and sisters across the country. The time may have come out of hours that could more reasonably be used for sleeping. However, Solanus saw it as time well spent. He was very attached to his family. Some of his long letters were by now going out of the country. In the thirties, Solanus's brother Monsignor Edward, nine years his junior, had left his teaching post at St. Thomas College in St. Paul, Minnesota, to become a missionary in the Philippines.

In 1936, Father Maurice Joachim Casey, then sixty-nine, had begun to confide in Solanus his deep and growing disappointment with a few Capuchin superiors who had been cautious about a background of instability in him. Maurice was to live with Capuchin friars but was only under the authority of the house superior where he was living. He was also free to keep his own money, since he had not taken the vow of poverty. But even with his freedom, Father Maurice Joachim was becoming increasingly distressed and depressed.

In the summer of 1936, Solanus went to New York to see

Maurice. His brother was assigned to parish work at Our Lady of Sorrows Parish in Manhattan. Father Maurice was also celebrating the twenty-fifth anniversary of his ordination in June. Our Lady of Sorrows was familiar ground for Solanus. This parish had been his second assignment, and a very unique one. Those three years represented a time of great spiritual peace and growth for Solanus. When Father Solanus arrived, he discovered how troubled his older brother was becoming in that same house. Maurice was disgruntled because his superiors did not wish to adopt a plan he had developed for promoting prayer. Solanus noticed that Maurice had made many friends and was doing well pastorally in Manhattan. But in the eyes of Father Maurice Joachim, the painful parts of life were overshadowing the joys and successes.

Some months later Father Solanus greeted a letter received from Maurice with great enthusiasm. St. Joseph Church at Prescott, Wisconsin, near the first Casey homestead, was celebrating its seventy-fifth jubilee in the summer of 1937. Maurice had asked Father Solanus if he could break away from St. Bonaventure's for a week to go with him to the celebration. Maurice also explained that he also asked Monsignor Ed if he could come for it from the Philippines. It would be a time they could all spend together, Father Maurice added.[10]

Father Solanus needed no coaxing to consider the idea. He believed that it would be good to spend time with his brothers — brothers by blood and brothers in ordination. And he knew that the experience might be of special benefit in helping Maurice to forget his heartaches for a while. Solanus found a few minutes late one evening to write to Ed, urging him to return from the Philippines for the trip if he could.

Finally, the three Caseys met in Chicago one summer day and headed for western Wisconsin. Father Solanus wore a black suit with Roman collar for the first time. The Capuchin rule had been changed and he thought it would be more comfortable for travel than the Capuchin habit. He felt strange in the suit. Later, he asked Maurice and Ed if his beard, spread down over his chest and over his collar, made him look more like a Jewish rabbi than a Roman Catholic priest.[11] The three chuckled over that. In August, they drove through the farmlands and valleys, trying to identify places they had not seen in decades. Father Solanus met priests who had studied with him at St. Francis' diocesan seminary in the 1890s.

At Trimbelle, the brothers toured the parish where they had received religious training and where Monsignor Edward Casey had been baptized. The three met up with eighty-three-year-old Alex Hupert who'd bought the Casey farm from Bernard Casey, Sr., when the family moved on to Burkhardt, Wisconsin, in 1882. Overjoyed to see the Casey sons who were now priests, old Alex invited them to come out to have dinner and to see the place again the next day. Monsignor Edward joked that he would love to, in return for the nostalgic joy of pitching bundles of hay — a job he'd done often as a young man. Solanus laughed and said that he simply wanted to walk the farm he'd lived on as a boy.

On the day of the visit, Fathers Solanus and Maurice and Monsignor Edward stopped to visit the graves of their little sisters, Mary Ann and Martha. It was the first time that Solanus and Edward had ever visited their graves. Edward was born after their deaths and Solanus had been very sick with diphtheria himself when both little girls had died.

Solanus found the place familiar but different. He saw the area where the Caseys had often seen deer moving past bushes along a ravine. Now the bushes were overwhelmed by trees and the fields were so overgrown that he could no longer see the hill he'd climbed often. On another hill overlooking the spring was the shell of the cabin the Caseys had once fondly called their "new house." Only the cellar was left. A thirty-foot oak had also grown up right in the middle of where the cabin once stood.[12]

The entire adventure of this "return to roots" was later retold for brothers and sisters in a long letter Solanus wrote. Seventeen pages in length, it was like a diary account of this late summer excursion. Solanus wanted to share the joys of the trip with his entire family, but it was sent, first of all, to his oldest brother, Jim. At the time, Jim was sick. Solanus did the next best thing he could do to taking Jim along.

It was also in 1937 that Father Solanus was asked to deliver a five-minute talk on a Detroit radio station. The city saw that the worst years of the Great Depression were over. It seemed to be a good time to say "thank you" to the Capuchins for their lifesaving charity to the needy. Though Father Solanus was still only the monastery porter and certainly did not have a resonant voice, there seemed to be no better spokesman for the Capuchins of the city. Solanus himself had great respect for the medium of radio. He was a friend and admirer of Father Charles Coughlin, the "radio priest" from nearby Royal Oak who was very popular then.

The radio talk by Father Solanus had no political message that would have reminded his listeners of Father Coughlin. It was set up in conjunction with an appreciation program put on by the cities of Detroit and Windsor, Ontario, across the Detroit River in Canada. It wasn't a surprise to those who knew him that Father Solanus used this occasion honoring the Capuchins to thank others outside the order.

He thanked the bakers who'd donated bread, the farmers who'd given vegetables, and the butchers who'd supplied meat bones for those hundreds of pots of soup. Solanus also thanked the many benefactors who'd donated funds to help subsidize the Capuchin soup kitchen. It was a simple talk, and Detroit people listening to the high-pitched voice of Solanus must have smiled. Solanus rarely accepted thanks for what he gave. Passing along the praise for good works was utterly consistent with the man's style and spirituality.[13]

Meanwhile, Solanus was much less sure about what to say to his own brother Father Maurice Joachim. Having been transferred by the Capuchins to the order's seminary at Marathon, Wisconsin, in 1937, Maurice had grown more dissatisfied with Capuchin life. Throughout that year and 1938, he was considering leaving the order to return to the diocesan priesthood. Father Solanus was kind but blunt about his views of such an attempt. Solanus wrote him that the diocese which Maurice had left to become a Capuchin could hardly be expected to welcome back a seventy-one-year-old priest who was unhappy. But Father Maurice Joachim was beyond listening to such counsel. Emotionally disturbed, he could no longer hear his brother, a man so many people took great pains to consult.[14]

One day in 1938, the pastor of St. Paul's Maltese Parish, Father Michael Z. Cefai, was sitting in the provincial superior's office at St. Bonaventure. Father Cefai had just been explaining his need for a priest to help with Masses at his parish on the weekends. Father Marion Roessler, the superior, had been looking over the list of men still available to assign for weekend duty. It didn't look encouraging, Father Cefai said years later.

Then Father Marion admitted that he had a few older priests left, including Father Solanus Casey, except that Father Solanus wasn't "allowed to go out, does not hear confessions and can't speak Maltese."

At just that moment, Father Solanus happened to come into the office on another matter, Father Cefai recalled. When told of the reason for Father Cefai's visit, Father Solanus immediately volunteered for weekend help at St. Paul's, if Father Marion approved. And so Father Solanus began to go to St. Paul's each weekend to say Mass. He continued to do so every week until 1942, and occasionally until 1945. Doing so added to the strain on him. Very quickly, people flocked to him at the parish in the same way that they descended upon St. Bonaventure's.[15]

Finding it hard to say no, Father Solanus, with the permission of Fathers Cefai and Marion, began to stay after the Masses to counsel people. Hundreds came to St. Paul's to see him during those hours when he was theoretically free of the task back home at St. Bonaventure's.

From all that he heard and saw, Father Solanus was deeply disappointed with the Roosevelt administration. "I say God bless him, too," Solanus wrote to his sister Margaret, "though my enthusiasm for him is almost, or fast becoming ancient history."[16] In his eyes, little seemed to be done for the poor and the hungry. The lines at the soup kitchen were just as long or longer in 1937 as they had been in 1929. Detroit's picture seemed to be no better. Automobile production, the city's "bread and butter," did not recover its 1929 levels until 1948.[17]

Throughout 1937 and 1938, Father Solanus felt a need to consult with his brother Monsignor Edward. Edward had stayed on in the U.S. after the trip to western Wisconsin. He was commissioned to raise funds for the Philippine missions. But his travels left him free to visit his brother Solanus from time to time. The two discussed Maurice and how they might help him.

For his part, Father Maurice was by then suffering physically as well as psychologically. A painful carbuncle, or boil, on the back of his neck was giving him some trouble. Doctors in Marathon did not know how to treat it. When the Capuchin superiors sent Maurice to clinics in the Fond du Lac area, the results were no more encouraging.

Father Maurice Joachim apparently became disgusted with his Capuchin community which could not even help him find healing for a boil on the back of his neck. Perhaps he was also offended that his own brother Solanus, who was so well known for his gift of healing, could not or would not help him. In any case, Maurice left his Capuchin residence at Marathon and went to visit Father Charles Coughlin in Royal Oak, a Detroit suburb. There seemed to be no plan for his life, other than to "leave the Capuchins."

Only when Father Coughlin urged Maurice to call Solanus did Father Solanus learn that his older brother was nearby. Solanus talked with him and agreed to arrange a meeting between Maurice and the provincial. The meeting took place and Maurice received what he wanted — a letter of exit from the Capuchins.[18]

Just what effect all of this had on Father Solanus can only be imagined. He surely talked with Monsignor Edward about the whole situation until Ed returned to his missions. Solanus was close to seventy years of age himself. Seeing Father Maurice Joachim searching aimlessly for fulfillment in his priesthood was surely painful to his family. Yet, it may have been more difficult for Father Solanus than for any of the other Caseys. It was Solanus's example which had inspired Maurice to try the seminary a second time. And it was to the Capuchins, the order Solanus chose, that Maurice had once been drawn.

Nonetheless, there was little that anyone could do to guide Maurice or to console his worried family. For a while, it wasn't clear just where Maurice was. Then Solanus was informed that Maurice was at the Mt. Hope Sanitarium in Baltimore. During the summer of 1940, the Molloy family of Detroit drove Solanus east to visit Maurice. For two weeks, the brothers spent time together. Solanus may have needed the trip away as much as Maurice needed to see his brother. In the spring of 1940, the assistant porter had been sick for weeks with colds and flu made more persistent probably by fatigue.[19]

In the world at large, there was little news that would have given peace of mind to seventy-two-year-old Father Maurice in Baltimore. In Europe, British and French troops were already at war with Germany. As did other Americans, the Capuchins followed the grim chain of global events. As Franciscans committed to peace, the men at St. Bonaventure Monastery renewed and redoubled their commitments to prayer. The electricity bill for lights in the chapel edged up as the threat of war increased.

In the autumn of 1939, Germany had invaded Poland, a country that had alliances with Great Britain and France. As President Franklin D. Roosevelt had watched the progress of war over the preceding twelve months, he had become privately convinced that the U.S. could not remain neutral indefinitely. Publicly, however, he swore that his presidency would not send American men onto battlefields. Right after his third election in 1940, however, President Roosevelt said that the U.S. would supply war matériel to nations at war with Germany and Italy. Everyone knew that this would involve the U.S. in the war sooner or later.

On Sunday, December 7, 1941, the Capuchins at St. Bonaventure heard about the surprise attack by Japan at Pearl

Harbor in Hawaii. The Japanese had attacked at 7:55 A.M., a time when the warships were in the harbor and planes were on the ground. Twenty-three hundred American servicemen were killed in the bombing and strafing. President Roosevelt went to a joint session of Congress the next day and asked for a declaration of war against Japan.

December 8 was also the Feast of the Immaculate Conception. For almost a century and under that title, Mary had been patroness of the United States. The Capuchins and many others saw the feast day "declaration of war" as a sign that the U.S. should seek the special protection of Mary as the U.S. entered World War II.

With the coming of war, the Great Depression came to an end. The economy became a wartime economy as factories were adapted to produce war goods. Detroit went back to work making jeeps, trucks, and tanks while hundreds of the city's men went to war. At St. Bonaventure's, the soup lines began to get shorter, although the Capuchins never did close the soup kitchen they'd opened in 1929.

While the rhythm of life was radically altered by war in almost every part of the world, the life of prayer at St. Bonaventure remained the same. Though his working hours were longer, the routine for Father Solanus Casey was not very different than it had been twenty years earlier. He rose, often before 4:30 A.M. Within the city, he had become a celebrity, a reality he found embarrassing.

One day, Solanus was visited by Steve Gergely of Detroit. The panic-stricken man begged Father Solanus to go to the hospital and bless his wife, Leona, who was near death. She had contracted pneumonia after surgery. Father Solanus could not go. He was on his way to say Mass, but he took off a medal of St. Theresa and told Steve to pin it on Leona. The nurses and Mr. Gergely saw a change for the better immediately.[20]

Not every request got such undivided attention, however. During this period, one woman from Detroit called Father Solanus on the phone often. The friary phone was near his desk and answering it was part of his responsibilities as porter.

One day, Solanus took the call, listened to the woman, made a few comments, and then hooked the receiver on the wooden shelf just above his desk. Then he proceeded to talk with the visitor on the other side of his desk. Every few minutes or so, he would take the phone, listen, make a remark, and put the receiver down again. After a while, he noticed that everyone was observing this charade. After he picked up the phone the next time, he grinned and silently mouthed the words. . . SHE'S STILL TALKING![21]

People came and left St. Bonaventure's Monastery on Mt. Elliott Avenue in astounding numbers. Sometime in 1940, Mrs. Martha Casey, the wife of Solanus's brother Owen, stopped to visit at St. Bonaventure. Solanus had never met the lady and took time to entertain her until he had to return to his desk. A young Capuchin brother came in to talk with Mrs. Casey instead. After a while, Martha asked the brother how many people came to see Father Solanus on an average day.

The brother guessed that Father Solanus typically saw between one hundred fifty to two hundred people each day at St. Bonaventure's. Most of them came simply to ask him for a blessing — a momentary visit. But from forty to fifty others came to talk with him at some length about a problem, illness, or grief.[22] As the wartime draft took more and more men to war, those who had loved ones in the armed forces came to ask prayers for their men.

In June of 1941, a Detroit man named Luke Leonard showed up to talk with Solanus. Leonard was well known in the city's real estate circles, but he was fighting a war that never had coverage in any newspaper. Leonard was battling alcoholism and was losing the battle. He had tried to taper off but wasn't able to wean himself from the bottle. Finally, on a Sunday morning after having had no alcohol for several days, the man walked over to St. Bonaventure's. He was feeling desperately ill and was shaking all over.

Father Solanus apparently recognized immediately that Leonard's need for help was urgent. The porter finished talking with a couple and then approached Leonard, who told him that he wanted to talk privately. Inside a private room, Solanus asked when Luke Leonard had recovered from his "illness." The word "illness" and the priest's attitude of quiet encouragement impressed Leonard. He also noticed that Father Solanus seemed to believe that the "illness" was already over, that the battle was won.

"You mean my drunk, Father?" Leonard replied.

Solanus laughed quietly and then talked to the man for quite a while, though others were also waiting outside to talk with him. Luke Leonard left the friary encouraged. He never again had an alcoholic drink, he said years later. He believed that the spiritual support of Father Solanus had helped to cure his "illness."[23] Perhaps Solanus understood more about alcoholism than Luke Leonard realized. Many doctors and health authorities now believe that alcoholism is actually a disease, an "illness" as Solanus put it.

Inside the house, the Capuchins became almost accustomed to excited reports of blindness healed, deafness cured, atheism reversed. The friars themselves, however, were only rarely the recipients of the "favors" which continued to be linked with their aging porter Solanus.

Father Solanus believed that he and his brother Capuchins — and all others in religious life — were not to seek healings. If they were following closely in the footsteps of Christ, sufferings were to be seen as blessings. But there were a few Capuchins who were apparently relieved of some burdens through the prayers of Father Solanus. One was Brother Daniel Brady. He developed a serious infection in the jaw while in the novitiate in 1941. The situation was worrisome, he told Father Solanus, but not just because he was to have surgery.

Brother Daniel was anxious because major surgery would probably force his withdrawal from the novitiate and possibly put a halt to his religious vocation. Father Solanus understood. He instructed the young man to kneel and blessed him right then and there. "As he did so, he touched my cheek and when he did, I knew it was healed," Brother Daniel wrote of the event in 1983. "I could feel it tighten up."

When the brother returned to his dentist, there was no sign of the dangerous infection. Feeling as though he'd received a new lease on life, Brother Daniel breezed through the front door on his trip back from the dentist. Bubbling with his good fortune, he shared the news with Solanus at his desk.

"That calls for a celebration," Father Solanus agreed. Then, according to Daniel, the porter grinned, yanked open a desk drawer, and produced two intact ice-cream cones — one for himself and one for Brother Daniel. A visitor had come in with them a full thirty minutes earlier. In some inexplicable way, the cones had been "preserved" from their otherwise predictable and sloppy fate![24]

Father Solanus had always had a lively appetite for fun. But he had an unending taste for quiet and meditation, too. To those coming to see him, it seemed that Father Solanus often moved into a zone of deeper prayer after they told him of their problems. Solanus, they said, would lean back into his chair for a moment and gaze off into a new direction. He was quiet then and would respond only after spending some time in that realm. Often, he would then make prophetic sorts of statements or give counsel.

This was momentary meditation. Father Solanus had discovered that his ministry needed the nourishment of much meditation. That was why his hours of rest and sleep were increasingly diminished throughout the 1930s and 1940s. It was his choice. He felt more need to feed his spirit than to rest his body. Ironically, only illness began to provide Father Solanus with the bigger blocks of time for the prayer that he hungered for. Throughout the early 1940s, there were scattered bouts of illness, as the monastery chronicle noted. "September 13, 1942: Father Solanus was sick in bed last night; he was unable to go to his help-out at St. Paul's. Father Solanus was taken to St. Mary's Hospital with a 104.5 degrees temperature."[25]

The problem this time was a chronic case of eczema, a skin disease marked by itching, inflamed, and scaly skin. The legs of Father Solanus were severely inflamed by the eczema and were often almost raw.

On the night of September 12, trying a suggested remedy, he used the heat of an electric light near his feet, but he forgot to apply salve after turning off the light. By the morning of September 13, his legs and feet were unbearably painful and were beet-red. His fever went to 104.5 degrees and he was hospitalized at St. Mary's Hospital for about ten days. With that kind of fever and with the potential for infection, the situation was life-threatening.

It wasn't long before the people of Detroit heard that Father Solanus Casey was hospitalized. A rumor that he had died added to the deluge of calls and visitors the hospital had to handle. For Solanus, however, the illness was a time for penance and prayer, although a very painful time. It was a number of weeks before he could resume his full schedule at the porter's desk.

"To me it seemed about ten days of the really best penance that the poor sinner Solanus had ever gone through," Solanus wrote to his brother Jim. "The old foot is still stiff but by keeping it raised and rested, it causes very little pain," he wrote in another letter to his sister Margaret LeDoux.[26]

By late 1942 and early 1943, there was no way for Father Solanus to reassure his brother Monsignor Edward about his health. Edward had returned to the Philippines. Though his family could only guess at his fate, Monsignor Casey was imprisoned by the Japanese when the islands were overrun during World War II. Solanus and the rest of the Caseys continued to pray for Ed, not knowing whether he was dead or alive. Though he missed Edward's input, Father Solanus continued to monitor the welfare of Father Maurice in Baltimore through letters and phone calls. In the midst of that, Solanus learned that his seventy-eight-year-old brother, Jim, who had been in poor health for some years, had died in Seattle on January 12, 1944.

As a sort of prayer for his family, but especially for Maurice, Father Solanus began to reread *The Mystical City of God* by Mary of Agreda. It was a devotional work which he had become increasingly attached to since first reading it in

1924. Solanus recommended the four-volume work to many people over the years. The extreme length of the work (some six hundred pages for the first three volumes, nearly eight hundred for the fourth) and its questionable value in the eyes of some priests was about to create some controversy and some heartbreak.[27]

Some Capuchins asked Solanus whether he really believed that he was counseling people to read a worthy work. Solanus remained convinced of its value. Finally, however, in 1943 and 1944, the Capuchin superiors began to insist that Father Solanus separate himself from a group of supporters who had become extremely attached to him and to *The Mystical City of God.*[28]

The Capuchins did not wish to foster any sort of "personality cult" and they apparently believed that Solanus was being manipulated. It was time to protect both the man and the man's health.

On November 25, 1944, Father Solanus glanced at the calendar and realized that it was his seventy-fourth birthday. Silently, he thanked God for the blessings of all those years, but his day at the monastery brought no further thought of the anniversary.

New Year's Day of 1945 dawned just a few weeks later and the future looked brighter than it had for many years. The end of the war appeared to be coming. In Europe and in Asia, American soldiers were achieving victories along with the other Allied forces, while Germany, Italy, and Japan were weakening.

This retouched photo of Ellen (née Murphy) and Bernard Casey, Father Solanus's parents, was taken around 1890. The future couple met in the United States in 1860 after emigrating from Ireland during the Great Potato Famine. They were married in Salem, a suburb of Boston, Massachusetts, moved to Wisconsin two years later (where they lived for thirty years), and eventually ended up in Seattle, Washington.

The Casey clan posed for this family portrait on August 14, 1892, in Superior, Wisconsin. In front, starting from left, are: John, Margaret, Mrs. Casey, Genevieve, Mr. Casey, Grace, Thomas, and Maurice. In the back row, same order, are: Edward, Leo, Bernard (the future Father Solanus), James, Ellen, Patrick, Owen, and Augustine. Two other children, Mary Ann and Martha, died in childhood in 1878.

The Capuchins of Sacred Heart Parish pose with some of the students who resided at the school run by the Capuchins in Yonkers, New York. This photo, taken about 1912, shows Father Solanus in the middle of the back row.

Father Solanus (far right, back row) poses with the altar boys he shepherded at Sacred Heart Parish in Yonkers, around 1912.

This photo, taken in 1913 in Seattle, shows the three Casey brothers who became priests. From left: Father Maurice (ordained in 1911), Father Edward (ordained in 1912), and Father Solanus (ordained in 1904).

Bernard and Ellen Casey are shown surrounded by their sons and daughters, sons-in-law and daughters-in-law, and grandchildren, when the couple celebrated their golden wedding anniversary on October 6, 1913, in Seattle.

Chatting at the entrance to St. Bonaventure Friary, Mt. Elliott Avenue, Detroit, Michigan, around 1937, are a Capuchin friar and a visitor. Just inside the door and off to the side, Father Solanus used to serve as porter, answering the door and telephone while meeting and praying with thousands of people over the years. He served at St. Bonaventure's from 1924 to 1945. (The main entrance to St. Bonaventure Church is shown at left.)

This scene in the Capuchin soup kitchen in Detroit was photographed in 1939. Heeding one of the corporal works of mercy — that of "feeding the hungry" — are, from left (behind the diners): Fathers Solanus Casey, Salesius Schneweis, Gerard Hesse, Crescentian Volpel, and Matthias Nack. In front of the tables is Father Theodosius Foley. Some fifteen hundred to three thousand people were fed daily at this facility during the Great Depression.

Posing for the photographer at the entrance to St. Bonaventure's in Detroit, about 1939, are, from left: Father Alphonse Heckler (main porter), Brother Francis Spruck (tailor), and Father Solanus (assistant porter).

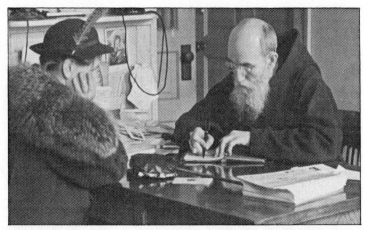

A visitor watches intently as Father Solanus enrolls her in the Seraphic Mass Association at the large oak desk he used near the main entrance of St. Bonaventure's. This picture was taken around 1939.

Along with a hearty bowl of soup and a beverage, the Capuchins figured on feeding the hungry about half a loaf of bread per person per meal. Loading up bread on a visitor's tray in this 1942 photo by the Detroit News *are, from left: Father Matthias Nack, an unidentified Third Order member, and Father Solanus Casey.*

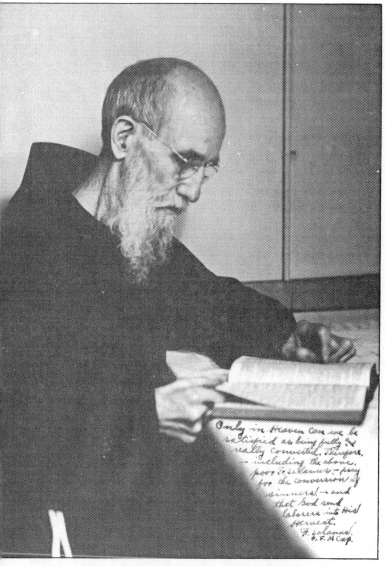

A message on a 1943 photo given to Edward and Selina Wollenweber of Detroit by Father Solanus reads: *"Only in Heaven can we be satisfied as being fully and really converted. Therefore, — including the above, poor Fr. Solanus — pray for the conversion of sinners — and that God send laborers into His Harvest. Fr. Solanus, O.F.M. Cap."*

On June 8, 1944, at the age of seventy-three, Father Solanus sat for this formal portrait taken by Brother Leo Wollenweber, O.F.M. Cap., showing him with his Bible.

While he often helped to feed others, Father Solanus (second from left in this picture probably taken in the late 1940s) was occasionally a very welcome guest at parish and Catholic organization dinners.

The celebration of Father Solanus's golden jubilee as a
Capuchin priest was the occasion for this gathering in Detroit
of part of the Casey clan in early 1947. From left: Owen Casey
of Seattle; Monsignor Edward Casey of St. Paul, Minnesota;
Father Solanus (then residing at St. Felix Friary in
Huntington, Indiana); and Mrs. Bernard (Grace, née Casey)
Brady, also of Seattle.

Playing the violin was a favorite form of relaxation for Father Solanus. Although he was not a gifted musician, he enjoyed playing such tunes as "Mother McCree," "Pop Goes the Weasel," and "Turkey in the Straw." This picture was shot at St. Felix Friary in Huntington in 1952.

Father Solanus chats with a visitor at St. Felix Friary in Huntington. Although he was supposedly retired, he continued his "front door ministry" of spiritual counseling and healing for more than fifty years — from 1904 to 1956, the year before his death.

With St. Felix Friary in Huntington as a backdrop, Father
Solanus poses for the Detroit News photographer in 1956 when
he was eighty-five years of age.

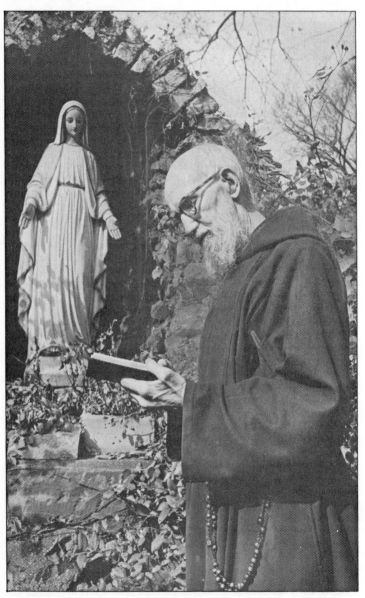

Father Solanus, in this 1956 Detroit News *photo, is shown reading and meditating on the Little Office of the Blessed Virgin Mary at the grotto in the St. Bonaventure Friary garden in Detroit.*

Father Solanus takes a moment to pray before a Nativity scene. During the Christmas season he loved to play carols on his violin before the crèche in the friary chapel. Though growing increasingly ill and weak, he continued the tradition even during his last Christmas, in 1956.

This is one of the last known photos taken of Father Solanus before his death on July 31, 1957. It was taken in the spring of that year.

Some twenty thousand people paid their last respects to Father Solanus, shown here in an open casket prior to his burial on August 3, 1957, in St. Bonaventure Cemetery.

Shown in this **Detroit News** *photo attending the funeral of Father Solanus are priests, brothers, and sisters from many different orders whose members had become friends with the Capuchin during his fifty-three years as a priest in the Order of Friars Minor.*

In this Michigan Catholic *photograph, a visitor relaxes after paying her respects at the original burial site of Father Solanus Casey before his remains were exhumed in the summer of 1987.*

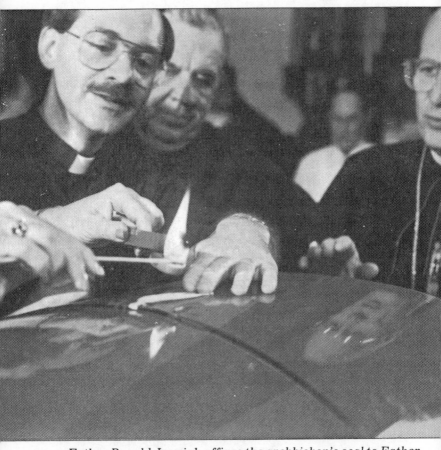

Father Ronald Jozwiak affixes the archbishop's seal to Father Solanus Casey's casket as Monsignor Albert Allen (directly behind Father Jozwiak) and Archbishop Edmund Szoka watch. This Michigan Catholic *picture was taken during the exhumation and reinterment of Father Solanus's body.*

This photo taken by Tom Ewald for The Michigan Catholic *shows Brother Leo Wollenweber — accompanied by a grandnephew and grandniece of Father Solanus, Dr. Michael Casey and Sister Anne Herkenrath, SNJM — standing over the new burial site of Father Solanus inside St. Bonaventure Church.*

CHAPTER NINE

Brooklyn and the Archangel's Wings (1945-1946)

In the spring and early summer of 1945, Americans were astir with great hope and a newborn confidence in the future. Many, though not all of the men and women who'd gone into the services to defend the nation, would be returning. The number of Americans listed as either killed or missing was 292,000.[1]

Even President Roosevelt, who had been president through much of the Great Depression and throughout the war years, was a sort of casualty of global war. After twelve years in office, he'd become exhausted and ill. He died on April 12 of a cerebral hemorrhage at the age of sixty-one. Three weeks later, on the seventh of May, Germany signed a statement of unconditional surrender. Despite the tragedies, peace seemed

148

as easy to smell as the spring blossoms and summer air that blew across the country.

The mood among members of the large Casey clan was similarly upbeat. There was good news about sixty-five-year-old Monsignor Edward in March. He had survived four years of imprisonment in a Japanese concentration camp in the Philippines. On March 23, the Americans stormed the camp before the Japanese had time to massacre their two thousand prisoners. Among the prisoners were one hundred twenty-five nuns, two bishops, and one hundred fifty priests, including Monsignor Casey. Led by the priests and bishops, many of the prisoners strong enough to do so had been praying hard for their freedom and survival.[2]

As the Casey family discovered later, their Monsignor Ed had acted courageously to protect weakened men just one day before American GIs rescued them. A Japanese officer had ordered calorie allotments to be cut from nine hundred to six hundred calories per day. It was a killing order. Even a nine-hundred-calorie daily regime was a terrible deprivation from the three-thousand-calorie daily requirement said to be optimal for men.

With immense pride in their brother Edward, the western Caseys decided to double their celebration plans for late June in 1945. John McCluskey, son of Patrick and Genevieve McCluskey of Seattle, was to be ordained. Genevieve was the youngest of the Casey sisters and brothers, nine of whom were still living.

The West Coast Caseys quickly decided that the occasion should be the largest, most joyous gathering of the Casey clan since the golden wedding anniversary of their parents in 1913. Now, war was ending. Their brother Edward had survived four years in a prisoner of war camp. There was to be a new priest in the family. There were reasons for Casey joy!

When Edward was back in the states, Owen and Patrick flew in from Seattle to welcome him. Together, the three brothers then traveled from Chicago to Detroit to see "Barney" at St. Bonaventure. At the monastery, they quickly urged him to accompany them on their trip west for the ordination of young John.

Solanus asked whether their brother Father Maurice was to accompany them as well. When Ed, Owen, and Pat said, "No," Solanus replied that he would not go if Maurice did not or could not go, pointing out that the oldest surviving Casey would be the only one not at the ordination. Solanus's resistance surprised the three younger brothers, but they knew there was no talking Solanus into going without Maurice.

Monsignor Edward, Owen, and Patrick Casey quickly boarded a plane bound for Baltimore. At Mt. Hope Sanitarium, they were finally able to arrange for the discharge of Father Maurice. Father Solanus and other family members had not been favorably impressed with the course of therapy for Father Maurice there anyway. A quick message to Father Solanus in Detroit was all the reassurance he needed. Solanus had already secured from his superiors permission for a vacation. In general, every friar was entitled to two weeks of vacation each year. Capuchin superiors at St. Bonaventure knew very well that, at seventy-four, Father Solanus could use a break from his grueling schedule.[3]

On June 15, reported the St. Bonaventure Chronicle, Father Solanus left for Chicago. There, he met with his four brothers. Together, Ed, Owen, Pat, Solanus, and Maurice boarded a train for the West. At the other end of the country, the Caseys, the LeDoux, the Bradys, and the McCluskeys waited in Seattle to gather the clan together once again.

None of the family had anticipated what the presence of Father Solanus would mean, however. Soon after Seattle people heard of his arrival, the phones began to ring and the living rooms began to fill with "visitors." Local pastors wanted Father Solanus to say Mass in their parishes. Father Solanus was a "celebrity" in a city where he had never even lived.

The story was the same in other places he visited. After young John's ordination at the end of June, Solanus went on to Spokane to visit other relatives there. Then relatives in California asked him to stay with them before returning to Detroit.

Thinking that he could get a train back to Detroit from Oakland or San Francisco, Father Solanus agreed.

Once in California, however, it was clear that travel was becoming a problem. The war had ended. Thousands of servicemen were coming into port in San Francisco on their way home. Father Solanus wrote to Father Marion Roessler, the guardian at St. Bonaventure, that he would not be able to return by the date indicated on his "obedience." The Capuchin superior in Los Angeles tried to help but to no avail. "So here I am still — hoping to make the best of missing the privileges of the Chapter," Father Solanus told Father Marion. Solanus also expressed a hope that the order of "discipline" would not suffer at the chapter.[4]

The "chapter" referred to a canonical meeting of superiors and delegates that met every three years to determine assignments, to elect new superiors, and to conduct other business of the order. This particular chapter was to make a very critical change with regard to its busiest porter, Solanus.

When Father Solanus was finally back in Detroit, it was already Saturday, July 21. He had been gone thirty-six days, or fifteen days longer than planned. The chapter had been concluded and a new superior at St. Bonaventure's, Father Bernard Burke, called him in to see him.

Solanus was quickly informed that he was being transferred. His new assignment was to be at St. Michael's Friary in Brooklyn. For twenty-one years, Solanus had been at St. Bonaventure's. He'd made hundreds of friends in Detroit; he'd grown used to but had not been defeated by the infirmities of old age in the Motor City. Father Burke noticed that Father Solanus received the news of this rupture most graciously.[5]

When he left Father Guardian, as the Capuchins referred to their superior, Solanus headed for his small room to pack a few things. He had very little time to make travel connections to New York. Capuchin regulations required that the friars be in place to begin new assignments within ten days of assignment announcements at the chapter. The chapter changes had been posted at 10:00 A.M. on July 15 while Father Solanus was still in California. He was bound by obedience to be at St. Michael's by ten in the morning on July 25. That gave him only two or three days to move.

This was certainly not the first time that Father Solanus Casey had been told to pull up his roots and relocate. It was, as he knew very well, part of religious life. It was also definitely part of the Franciscan spirit — no personal attachments, even to a city of people he'd loved so deeply through the years of the Great Depression and World War II. Nonetheless, there were people in Detroit who wondered, when they heard about his move, if such a transfer wasn't a bit hard on a man now in his seventy-fifth year.

In fact, it was his years and another concern that the Capuchin superiors had in mind in making the change.

In 1943-1944, the provincial leaders had become disturbed by some supporters of Father Solanus who had become devotees of *The Mystical City of God*. When people came to him seeking spiritual counsel, Father Solanus often recommended reading one or more volumes of the massive four-volume set. Some people did and became almost as devoted to the Agreda volumes as was Father Solanus. Others, on the other hand, felt differently about the Agreda work.

Eventually, officials at the Detroit chancery office were hearing complaints from some that a Capuchin was "promoting" a book which was not only expensive but also a burden to read. Besides that, in the eyes of some within the Church, Mary of Agreda's book was merely an apocryphal work and not at all worthy of endorsement by priests or other Church authorities.

A man named Ray Garland was at the center of *The Mystical City* devotees. He was also totally devoted to Father Solanus whom he had met in 1927. Later, when Father Solanus began to help out with weekend liturgies at St. Paul's Maltese Parish in Detroit, Garland and company followed. They attended the Masses Father Solanus had and also set up breakfast meetings after the Mass to study the Agreda volumes. But there was an intensity about the piety of this group that others saw as unhealthy. When Solanus was in the hospital and unable to attend their Sunday meetings, they continued to meet at St. Paul's themselves despite the wishes of the pastor that they meet only when Father Solanus was present for meetings.[6]

Father Solanus was finally ordered to tell Ray Garland not to come to St. Bonaventure's to visit. Though Father Solanus told his superiors that he felt Garland was being misunderstood, he was thoroughly obedient. But Garland apparently continued to telephone, short-circuiting the Capuchin superiors in a way Solanus found hard to rebuff. Garland was calling to seek the spiritual counsel of Solanus for himself and for the Agreda circle. Capuchin authorities finally believed that Father Solanus was being used without his being aware of it. In order to remove him from this "difficulty" and to give him a well-earned rest, he soon found himself on his way east to Brooklyn. He was to be porter — but in semiretirement — there at St. Michael's Friary.[7]

Before his Detroit friends knew that Father Solanus was back from California, he was already beginning to make himself at home at 225 Jerome Street in Brooklyn. When he looked around, Father Solanus quickly noticed the massive statue of St. Michael, a landmark near the church and friary. He described it to others as a very protective monument.

Though the news of his departure may have been devastating for many Detroit people who had come to know him, to many friars at St. Bonaventure's, the transfer of Father Solanus was just another transfer.

"It was kind of a surprise for the community and the people," recalled Father Cosmas Niedhammer, then novice master for the brothers' novitiate. "However, I was hardly conscious of it. I know he was simply told to go, and went. I know the rest of the community hardly noticed either."[8]

But if many of his Capuchin brothers hardly noticed the departure of Father Solanus, St. Michael's knew that something was very different within a month. Father Solanus, meanwhile, had to become reacquainted with the concept of "relaxing." In a note back to St. Bonaventure's written soon after he was established at St. Michael's, he confided that he'd been worn out and was relieved to move.

Solanus also wrote back to St. Bonaventure to Brother Leo Wollenweber, a young brother in his early twenties who'd been named to help with portering duties in the early 1940s. Solanus asked him to send along a few personal belongings he'd had no time to pack. Among the things he wanted sent was a copy of a small prayer he hoped to have duplicated for distribution to those wanting it.

"I hope to get a little more time for such things here at St. Michael's," Father Solanus told Brother Leo on July 30. "I've taken a little more sleep under the great archangel's wings this past week than perhaps in three weeks before my arrival." The weeks Solanus was thinking of were those busy weeks he'd spent visiting, meeting, and counseling people out west while he was "on vacation"! Within eight days, he had spanned the width of the country, traveling up and down the West Coast and then on to St. Paul, Detroit, and finally to New York.

Before long, however, friends from Detroit learned of his whereabouts. Some began to write to him, others planned to travel the six hundred miles to Brooklyn just to talk with him. A Mrs. Edward Wolfe, of Brighton, Michigan, felt she couldn't wait to do either. She called.

Doctors had told Mrs. Wolfe that her baby daughter, Kathleen, was suffering from celiac disease, an ailment in which food is incompletely absorbed in the intestines, thus contributing to malnutrition. Little Kathleen was literally starving to death despite her mother's best efforts to feed her. The doctors had nothing more to offer the child.

When Father Solanus had heard enough of the story from Mrs. Wolfe over the phone, he asked her to kneel down holding the baby in one arm. Solanus then blessed the baby "over the phone." He also asked her mother to spend the money she would have spent in coming to Brooklyn to do something for those in need. Soon, Baby Kathleen's disease started to regress. She began to digest food normally and was on the road to recovery.[9]

With little in the way of official responsibilities, Solanus did some sightseeing and visiting in the autumn of 1945. New York parishes, after all, had been his first assignments as a priest. He'd grown to love the city people. He returned to Sacred Heart for the annual Labor Day picnic. Solanus still loved the hot dogs with onions, the beer, the games that were part of the parish festival fun. There were a few who'd heard of the seventy-four-year-old from his years of ministry there before the First World War.

But back at St. Michael's, the hours of leisure disappeared as summer cooled and autumn overtook it. If there were fewer people to meet and talk with at St. Michael's door, there were many more to counsel by mail and over the phone. Every night, Solanus took pen in hand and wrote to as many people as his tired eyes and head could permit. Often, he did not quit until after midnight.

Little stacks of three-by-five postcards, his customary stationery, would be filled up with his responses often written in green ink, a Casey family preference. They were mailed out the next day, but that did not mean that Father Solanus had reached the bottom of his pile of "letters to be answered." That reality was very frustrating to him.

"I must be about fifty letters behind — quite some not opened," he wrote to his sister Margaret in Oakland. "Pray the Lord give some system or other whereby I keep up."[10] Among those letters Father Solanus had to answer was a pack from Ray Garland and the Agreda group in Detroit.

"I must tell you something that, in a way, I do not like to do," Father Solanus wrote to him, trying to broach a painful subject in a considerate fashion. "It is this. The arch-enemy of our Blessed Mother and of immortal souls — at all times on the alert — must have received an extra length of rope these days. I have been reported as having been phoning long distance to you and the 'Agredan Society.' "

The situation was giving "offense, if not scandal" to his Capuchin superiors, Father Solanus explained to Ray Garland. Because of that, he asked Garland to "leave me out of the picture" until all the misunderstandings were cleared up.[11]

It was, most probably, a painful message for Father Solanus to write. He was never convinced that the Garland group was at all misled in their interest in *The Mystical City of God*. But Father Solanus was obedient to the orders of his superiors and always ready to listen to their advice. The Garland connection was severed.

If Father Solanus was bothered by the forced end of this friendship, he did not show it. In fact, he worked hard at establishing a rapport with the Capuchins at St. Michael's. To some degree, his reputation as a priest of great virtue and great spiritual ministry had preceded him. But that was not enough to endear him as a musician during recreation time.

"Solanus decided to entertain the friars at their regular Sunday recreation time. So he came in with his violin. The friars thought, 'Well, he is an old man trying to entertain us.' So they put up with his squeaking on the violin. Their reaction seemed so positive to Solanus that he thought he had done very well. The next Sunday night he showed up with his violin again. As he began to play, one of them went to the radio and kept turning up the volume. Without saying a word, Solanus left the room and went down before the Blessed Sacrament and continued his playing" there.[12]

Perhaps Father Solanus should not have been surprised. His "virtuosity" with the violin had never earned him much respect. Even his brothers had complained when he'd taken up the fiddle as a youngster. Apparently, he'd never gotten any better at it, except possibly in the all-accepting eyes of heaven.

Fiddling hymns in the chapel provided a respite from the increasing burden of correspondence and visitors which Father Solanus found facing him in the autumn and winter months of 1945. He did find enough time during the winter to write some of his friends and send them a small Christmas verse he had composed years earlier. It was entitled "Always Christmas Eve." The short verse suggested that the heart of each man and woman could become a "crib" which receives the infant.

With love and Christmas greetings to all
Comes the Infant once more to free us from sorrow
Whose smile and whose power and whose gentleness call
To each heart and each soul for a manger tomorrow;

Whose love and whose goodness — whose wonders
        proclaim
Him, the Son of the Virgin, as promised of yore.
Oh, may he estrange us from sin and its shame!
And reign in our hearts, as his crib evermore!

Now he added this reflection:

. . . Ah, the rest of us, on Calvary
Mary conceived under the Cross
Thirty-three years later. Glory to God!
Peace to men of GOOD WILL.[13]

With World War II finally ended, Christmas of 1945 was a joyous one. In New York, Solanus sent out his Christmas verse with greetings and also tried to keep up with the increasing requests for his blessings and counsel. More and more, as the snow fell on Brooklyn, there were bundled-up visitors ringing the door at St. Michael's. And yet, he found the crush of visitors and the strain considerably less than it had been in Detroit.

"I do have perhaps hours as long but it's a change," Solanus wrote to his brother Edward. "Here it's correspondence that takes most of the time. There, I simply had to leave most of that to others. And while I meet with pathetic cases to solve or try to alleviate, the strain and tension is by no means so pressing."[14]

Over the years, Solanus had found a few ways to "escape" from the crush when the circumstances allowed for it. Serving as part-time porter at St. Michael's provided more of these opportunities to "escape."

Solanus would sneak a nap beneath the large porter's desk

when "business" was slow. Since he often did not go to bed until midnight and rose at 4:30 A.M. or so, the naps were not an old man's self-indulgence. If the phone rang or the doorbell buzzed, Solanus bounced up, dusted his habit off, smoothed his hair back into place, and resumed the dignified demeanor of a porter always at his post.

One of those who rang the bell at St. Michael's one day was the mother of Barnabas Keck, a Capuchin seminarian. He had met Solanus at the seminary in Garrison, New York. Mrs. Ruth Keck had already consulted someone about her problem. Her doctor had implied but refused to tell her that she was suffering from cancer. Her son later told the story of her meeting with Father Solanus.

"When my mother's turn came, Fr. Solanus said, 'And what's your problem, dear?'

" 'I think I have cancer,' she said.

"All he said was, 'Don't you know God can cure cancer just like a toothache?' So she knelt down and he put his hand on her and blessed her, praying over her."

She went home and never went back to the doctor and was eighty years old when the story was repeated in 1983.[15]

Such news traveled fast, especially in a large metropolitan area like New York. The lines of people waiting to talk with the porter at St. Michael's began to get longer and longer as the new year, 1946, began. Within six months of his arrival at St. Michael's, Capuchin superiors were already considering another transfer for Father Solanus Casey. They had suspected that St. Michael's wings might be only temporary shelter for Father Solanus. He would simply not have the chance to rest in a location like St. Michael's.

Transfers were amost always announced after the chapters, which took place every three years. But the superiors decided to place him immediately in a friary that would be farther from their larger metropolitan locations — friaries in Detroit, New York, Milwaukee.

On April 26, 1946, the chronicle, or log, of St. Michael's in New York noted that Father Solanus was being transferred to

St. Felix Friary in rural Huntington, Indiana. The Capuchins had moved their novitiate to St. Felix, which they had built in 1929. It was a friary surrounded by farmlands, and even within their own grounds the friars maintained their own orchard, vineyards, beehives, and a large vegetable garden.

Father Maurice Joachim had begun his own Capuchin novitiate there and Father Solanus had accompanied him there. After that, Solanus had been there on retreat or to get away from the Detroit routine. The superiors of Father Solanus felt relieved about this change. They seemed to think that life might slow down for Father Solanus there. They assigned him to complete retirement. His forty years as a porter had come to an end.

CHAPTER TEN

'Retirement' in Huntington (1946-1956)

Though he said nothing about it, in his heart of hearts Father Solanus Casey may have been relieved to hear the news of his transfer in April of 1946. Life at St. Felix would be close to farmlands and fields — and to God. Solanus could find a sermon in every square yard of ground. The handsome sprawling brick novitiate with Spanish tiled roof was surrounded by thirty acres of friary land.

Solanus had been born in a setting of wide-open spaces seventy-five years earlier. Most of his life, however, had been lived in large metropolitan areas. His superiors determined that it would be good to give the man a chance to enjoy the open air now that he was to be retired. On the other hand, they knew that Father Solanus was a man contented with whatever came; he was good at being a religious.

In keeping with the spirit of St. Francis, which saw each friar in the same fair light, the chronicle at St. Felix in Huntington made note of his coming in a very matter-of-fact manner. "April 25. Father Solanus arrived from St. Michael's, Brooklyn, with an obedience to be stationed here."[1]

By the time Father Solanus had settled in at St. Felix in the last days of April, spring was very much in the air. The Capuchin orchards were beginning to bud, promising a bountiful crop of apples, pears, peaches, and plums. But as the friary chronicle later noted, near the middle of May, Old Man Winter returned and threatened to ruin the crops. The friars, including the newcomer Solanus, were concerned.

"May 13. Father Dominic's mother died this evening," the recording friar noted. "Last Saturday when the daily papers announced the approach of frosts, the friars thought of lighting a smudge to save the tiny apples. Father Solanus volunteered to bless the orchard instead with the oration 'Ad Omnia' and one to Bl. Ignatius, Capuchin Brother. Now it appears that only the grapes froze. When all around us the neighboring apples were destroyed — ours were unharmed."[2]

Father Solanus had called upon the special protection of Blessed Ignatius of Laconi because that Saturday, May 11, was the feast of the good Capuchin brother. Five years after helping to "frost-proof" the apples at St. Felix, Ignatius was canonized.

If Solanus took some time to walk the grounds, most of his time was still occupied with correspondence. By May, much of what had been sent to St. Michael's in recent months was catching up with him.

"God bless you and yours," Father Solanus wrote, beginning a May 22 letter to a correspondent from Oswego, New York. "I hope this finds you well and that the 'kind of mixup' caused by my transfer hither, etc., may not be so grave as to be insurmountable."[3]

Solanus was aware that many in New York might have been disappointed that they could no longer visit him in Brooklyn — just as Detroiters had been distressed about his transfer to New York. Gradually, he had seen that a few people came not for his counsel on growing closer to the Lord, but for what Solanus could do *for* them. Solanus did not make a secret of the location of his new residence. His correspondence went out on friary notepaper, carrying the address "St. Felix Friary, Route 8, Huntington, Indiana." In general, however, the other friars at St. Felix understood that it was best to say little about the presence of Father Solanus Casey to those outside their house, as Solanus was there for retirement.

And yet, Solanus could admit that his "retirement" was still a bit taxing. "Since my transfer from St. Bonaventure's my personal callers have been by no means as heavy; though my letters — possibly because I have to take care of them myself — seem as heavy as ever; and you can imagine how I appreciate it to have someone like one of the Brothers or Fathers in Detroit continue their generous assistence [sic] in the work that, even with such help, often keeps me — with other duties — from 5 o'cl a.m. to 11 p.m."[4]

In late June, Solanus received word that his younger brother Augustine (Gus) had died in Seattle at the age of seventy. Later, he learned that two days before Gus died, he had been reconciled with his brother Patrick. For some time, there had been bitter feelings between the two. Father Solanus had urged both of his brothers to forgive and forget and the healing had apparently taken place.

Solanus was grieved over the loss of Gus and wished that he had been able to have more contact with him. Family relationships were very important to him. One of the burdens of his ministry had been the trouble he had in finding time to keep in touch with the large and active Casey clan. Fortunately, his new location in Indiana was more accessible for Maurice and Edward than Brooklyn had been. By now, Edward was based in Minnesota working for the Philippine missions. Father Maurice was in semiretirement, cheerfully serving as chaplain at a Catholic hospital in Graceville, Minnesota.[5]

In September, as the house chronicle indicates, Monsignor Edward and Father Maurice came down to visit Father Solanus at St. Felix. They stayed over and walked with Solanus through the orchards that Solanus had already glowingly described to his sister Margaret as "bountifully loaded." The seasons passed quietly in Huntington and the friars celebrated Advent and Christmas with great joy. In January, however, there was another reason to celebrate.

On Saturday, January 25, 1947, the *Detroit News*, a Detroit daily, printed a short article about Father Solanus. It announced that he was visiting the city from his new residence in Huntington, Indiana, in order to celebrate his fifty years as a Capuchin. He had entered the order on January 14, 1897. The *News* also stated that the major celebration of this anniversary would be held at St. Bonaventure's on the following day, Sunday, January 26.

Up until this printed announcement of his return to Detroit, few of his Detroit admirers even knew where he was living. Fewer still knew that his golden jubilee celebration was close at hand. The effect of the small announcement in the paper would not have been much greater if it had appeared in large type on the front page with a picture of Solanus!

St. Bonaventure's chapel was packed during the golden jubilee liturgy. Solanus noted the crowd with gratitude but could not help wandering back in memory to that cold January fourteenth in 1897. He'd walked into this same church. It was colder then, lacking the amenities of a more efficient heating system. He'd been kneeling, consumed with anxiety and doubts. He'd had knots in his stomach as he stood up to take off his suitcoat. Then the heavy brown hooded habit of these Capuchins had been placed over his head which at that time was still covered with plenty of dark hair. After receiving the new clothing, he'd been given his new name, "Frater Francis Solanus Casey." Right away, he also realized that he'd been given peace.

Solanus watched then as his brother Monsignor Edward mounted the pulpit to preach about Solanus's fifty years of service. Edward had told Solanus, his older brother, that his homily would be based on the Scripture verse "To those who love God, all things work together for good." Solanus leaned back to listen.[6]

After the liturgy, those attending were handed a small card which was given as a memento of the occasion. On the back was a message from Father Solanus. Solanus had written, polished, and changed it a dozen times. A nervous friar had stood nearby, anxious to get the text over to the printshop. The message read:

PAX ET BONUM
IN MEMORY OF MY
GOLDEN JUBILEE IN RELIGION

St. Bonaventure's Monastery
Detroit, Michigan
Thanks be to God for uncountable
mercies — for every blessing!
Thanks be to my neighbor for his
charitable patience.

Fifty years in the Order — almost unnoticed — have slipped away from me into eternity. Thither I hope to follow before half another fifty: trusting in the merciful goodness of God!

Fr. Solanus, O.F.M. Cap.

DEO GRATIAS

A dinner was held after the Mass to celebrate the event at the Third Order Hall, just down the block from St. Bonaventure's. The hall was filled to capacity. After the dinner, Father Solanus, Monsignor Edward, Father Maurice, their brother Owen, and their sister Mrs. Grace Brady went to a large room above the hall for a reception. More than two thousand people filed through a reception line, greeting, hugging, and giving money and gifts of all kinds to Father Solanus.[7]

The crowd that had assembled with so little publicity was awesome. Capuchin authorities, standing just out of the limelight occupied by Father Solanus, took note of the numbers. Father Solanus was better off in Huntington, a little farther from the hundreds and hundreds of people who knew him but also tired him.

Even in the reception line, many people were trying to update the guest of honor on the progress or difficulties in their lives. As always, Solanus listened keenly and did the best he could to respond. It took several hours before everyone crowding into the reception line had a chance to say a word or two to Father Solanus.

Two or three days later, Solanus, Ed, and Maurice saw their siblings Owen and Grace off to Seattle. Then on February 1, after his other guests had left, Father Solanus returned to Huntington, driven by his good friends from Chicago, Joseph and Winifred O'Donnell. The O'Donnell car also carried the many gifts given to Solanus. These included vestments, an alb, altar linens, money, and a chalice. Though Solanus appreciated the love and affection he received, he hardly knew what to do with the many gifts that people increasingly showered upon him. After asking permission, he later gave the chalice to a visiting missionary bishop serving in India.

Notice of his Huntington, Indiana, residence in the Detroit paper increased the numbers of visitors headed for Huntington. It also quickly doubled and tripled the mail coming into St. Felix Friary. Most of the friary's incoming mail was addressed to "Father Solanus Casey." Facing daily mini-mountains of mail, Father Solanus had taken up typing somewhere along the line. But his typing speed was poor and served primarily to spare his hands. As he had grown older, his hands had become more arthritic, making it hard for him to hold a pen.

His Huntington days typically started at 4:15 or 4:30 A.M., though the community was not awakened until the 4:55 sounding of the wooden clappers. The friar assigned to the task of awakening the others slapped the wooden blocks together, announcing *Surgite, Fratres* ("Arise, Brothers"). It had been the same daily awakening routine since Solanus had entered the order as Barney Casey, Jr., a half-century earlier.

After rising, Solanus would slip his habit over his head, pull on his sandals, and head for the chapel. He liked to pray alone there until the rest of the community gathered at 5:15 for morning prayers. A community Mass followed at 6:15. Afterward, there was breakfast. It was still eaten in silence. The strange practice Solanus still had of mixing his coffee, orange juice, and cereal into one strange-looking breakfast stew must have made the silence a challenge for the novices.

At 8:00 A.M., Solanus slipped into the chapel again to attend the Mass celebrated for the novices in residence and in schooling at St. Felix. After Mass, he lingered in prayer in the chapel until 9:15 or 9:30. That was the time the postman usually came with the sacks of mail from the Huntington Post Office.

By 9:30 in the morning, Solanus had already been up for over five hours. His workday started then as mail was opened and sorted. Much of the mail related to requests for enrollment in the Seraphic Mass Association for which Solanus was the friary director. There was money in many of the letters Solanus had to open. Not long after he returned from Detroit and his golden jubilee, Father Matthias, the Capuchin guardian, appointed Father Herbert to help Solanus with correspondence.

Father Ambrose De Groot, then about thirty-nine, was assigned to St. Felix in the summer of 1946. From what he heard, Father Solanus needed help badly.

"Naturally it was just too much for him to take care of all this correspondence. Money for Seraphic Mass enrollments and stipend money for Masses would frequently be found buried in the pile of mail on his desk. It wasn't that he was careless. He just wasn't a legalist so that he found reason to worry about these matters. . . . It even took Father Solanus forever just to write his name on an SMA card. Father Herbert also made replies to all these requests. But if the person sought any personal advice from Father Solanus, this, of course was left to him."[8]

If letters could be stacked up to be answered later, phone calls and visitors at the friary door could not be.

"The phone rang continually — and almost every time, the party at the other end of the line asked to speak with Father Solanus," Father De Groot recalled. "Sometimes we would have to search all over the grounds for him. Perhaps he would be out walking — or running around the orchard, which he loved to do for exercise. Old as he was, he was wiry and limber. The doorbell too was ringing constantly for him. Cars came from almost every state in the union and from Canada.

He took his time with each person who came to him. He listened to their problems. And undoubtedly he helped them. He must have done *something* for them. Or else his clientele would have faded out. But it didn't."[9]

When called away from what he was doing, Father Solanus, as the younger Father De Groot observed him, "never showed impatience or resentment. And . . . [his patience] must have been tried many times." Perhaps in response to the overload, Father Solanus escaped to "outdoor ministries." In the garden or on the lawn, he could be silent. It was very satisfying to tend to growing things, or to the beehives in which he took a special interest.

"Some bees arrived today from Dadant Co. in Illinois," noted the St. Felix chronicle for May 8, 1947. "Father Master and Solanus put them in their new home. Several weeks ago the old bees had been discontented with our hospitality and decided to pull up stakes for a better place. So they swarmed and left us empty-handed. When the new bees arrived, it was found that the queen was dead. Father Solanus immediately called the company and asked for another."[10]

Though he was going on seventy-seven, Father Solanus remained in relatively stable health during the summer of 1947. Around Huntington, he was occasionally seen visiting the Victory Noll Sisters, as Our Lady of Victory Missionary Sisters are popularly called. Founded by Father John Sigsteen — and subsequently supported by Archbishop John F. Noll, the bishop of the diocese and founder of the Catholic publishing house Our Sunday Visitor, Inc. — the Victory Noll Sisters had their motherhouse just two miles from the monastery.

Often Father Solanus would go with some of the other Capuchins to Victory Noll when they went to hear the confessions for the sisters. Solanus would simply sit and talk to the nuns, enjoying their company.

In June, Bernard Casey, a nephew of Father Solanus, came to visit for a few days from San Francisco. He'd been in the service during the war and wanted to get to know his uncle a little before settling in to civilian life.

In the autumn, Solanus was still active inside and outside the friary. While visitors and loads of letters preoccupied much of his day in his small office at St. Felix, he continued to hoe in the garden, attack weeds in the lawn, and serve as assistant beekeeper. In late December, however, the skin problem with his legs flared up again. This time, the house chronicle noted on December 31, the flare-up was vicious.

"We gave our annual spiritual bouquet to Father Guardian this evening after supper. Father Damasus gave the talk . . . and he surprised us all. It was very nice. Recreation this evening. Father Solanus has been ill for several days already. He has a skin disease on his legs. He could not say Mass this morning, and there seems little chance for immediate improvement. Seems to be getting worse."

The chronicler was making no overstatement. The ailments Father Solanus suffered from were becoming worse. His superiors could assume that his pain and discomfort had become acute when he admitted that he could not rise to say Mass. If there was any way to put up with his inflamed legs, Solanus would say Mass. By January 25, 1948, the chronicle added, "Father Solanus came to dinner today in the refectory — the first time in many days. He is feeling better but is still far from well."[11]

Even on the days before he was down for dinner, however, Solanus was doing what he could to get letters out. One went to his niece Mrs. Aurelia Herkenrath, who was experiencing problems with her hearing. Her uncle told her that he had enrolled her in the Seraphic Mass Association. His concluding words contained a familiar message: "I think it would help if you made a proposition to the Poor Souls — including your relatives specially — that you will enroll them most specilly [*sic*], say for a small % of the Dr. bill if your hearing improves without treatment so as to surprise the doctors. Then have as many as possible to offer holy communion often. Fr. Sol."[12]

By Holy Week, 1948, Father Solanus had rebounded again. On Good Friday, he served as subdeacon at services and as deacon at the Easter liturgy on Sunday, March 28. Within another ten days, he was able to watch Brother Harold plowing the fields outside. His fellow friars at St. Felix now had recognized a quick way to assess the condition of his legs. "If he ran up the stairs," one friar noted, "we knew he was feeling well, but if he seemed to lumber along, then we knew that his legs were giving him a lot of trouble."[13]

On June 6, Father Herbert, who had been helping Father Solanus, was getting ready to leave for Montana, but the Capuchins were not about to leave Solanus without an assistant. On June 9, Father Blase Gitzen arrived from Detroit. Newly ordained, Father Blase had served as an altar boy for Solanus many years earlier. He remembered Solanus as the very pious priest who always took so much longer to say Mass.

Father Blase was assigned to serve as full-time secretary for Father Solanus. With his young eyes and energy, it was hoped that much of the burden of the correspondence could be lifted from the aging, weakening shoulders of Solanus. Young Father Blase prepared to roll up his sleeves and roll paper into the office typewriter. However, he noticed right off that there were a few things askew which he wanted to straighten out.

"In some ways he offended my Prussian regularity and orderliness," Father Blase said of Father Solanus in an interview given many years later. "He had money on him (which he just stuffed into his habit pockets) and money all over the room (which he stuffed into the cubby holes of his desk, or used as page markers). And he didn't know to which account that money was to be credited.

"So one day, with the blessing of the superior, I went through his room and collected $153. He never said anything, but I got the impression that he wasn't very pleased that I cleaned up his room. Not that he cared about the money. He never took care of it because he just couldn't care less. But I lost his place in many a book!"[14]

During the summer of 1948, Father Blase also began to set up more of a routine for handling the incoming mail. He would open the thirty to forty letters which Solanus received each day. Blase would then record money received and sort the letters. In one stack were letters which he thought might require a simple acknowledgment. In the other stack, however, were the heart-wrenching stories of people desperate for some spiritual consolation and prayer. Blase "prayed" that Father Solanus would reply to these himself. And Solanus typically did.

"In the course of the day, I would receive the answers he had crashed out on an old battered typewriter. They were typed mostly on three-by-five cards. The spelling was bad, pure fifth-grade stuff, but the contents simply amazed me. With a few words he was able to come to the heart of the problem. His understanding of people, his sympathetic response, his grasp of theology just astounded me."[15]

In the late afternoon, Father Solanus and many of the other friars were working outdoors. Sometimes, Solanus was out after the dandelions in the lawn. But at other times, he was involved in more serious efforts. On July 27, as the chronicle reported, "Father Master with Father Solanus' help extracted 40 lbs. of honey from one of the hives."[16] The queen bee ordered by Solanus during the previous year had managed to get things going quite successfully.

Bees fascinated Father Solanus. He was often noticed by some of the other friars near the apiary. One or two bees were crawling up and down his welcoming fingers as he "preached" some sort of outdoor sermon to them. Occasionally, he was stung, but his admiration for the "marvelous things" wasn't diminished.

One time after finding a bee in his office, he coaxed the thing onto his finger and headed for the window to set it free. But Solanus found that the screen couldn't be budged. At just that moment, Frater Leon had the misfortune to pass by. Solanus called him in and transferred the bee to Leon's hand because Leon's legs were younger and quicker. Leon was a bit skeptical about escorting a bee but couldn't refuse Father Solanus. The young man made it down the corridor and almost to the outside friary door. Then, he got the bee's point![17]

In September of 1948, the house guardian, Father Matthias, died. A week later, Father Herbert (the Capuchin who had helped Father Solanus with his mail several years earlier) was named the new guardian. He knew very well how taxing the office work and visitors were on Solanus. The one-time porter was now almost seventy-eight years old. During the autumn and winter, however, Father Solanus remained in good health and was very active.

On January 12, 1949, Father Solanus received sad news. Monsignor Edward called to tell him that Father Maurice Joachim had died. Maurice was eighty-one years old. Coincidentally, Jim Casey, the oldest Casey son, had died on the same date, January 12, in 1944.

As a brother, Father Solanus felt the loss of Maurice keenly. He had suffered with the trials experienced by Father Maurice for many years. Through dozens of phone calls and hundreds of hours of letter-writing and talking, Solanus had tried to help Father Maurice find a joy and peace in the gifts God had given him.

As a believer, however, Solanus was happy for the new life Maurice could now enjoy. Up in Graceville, Minnesota, several days later, it was Father Solanus who gave the homily at his older brother's funeral liturgy. He spoke of death as a humiliating but purifying gateway to eternal life. Death, he told the congregation, "is the last of the blessings God showers upon our earthly journey toward home." It was his favorite theme — gratitude to God for whatever he gives to us.

Solanus himself was best suited to know how difficult that had been for Maurice. Maurice had suffered humiliations just to become a priest. He had failed in the seminary at an early age and had then returned after he saw Barney ordained. Later, Maurice had sincerely believed that he could serve best as a Capuchin. But even that assurance faded. He finally left the order and later felt misunderstood and frustrated as a priest. Clearly burdened by mental and emotional problems, Maurice had known very little peace until the very end of his life.

Soon after the funeral, Father Solanus sat one day in his

Huntington office and told a Detroit visitor, Miss Agnes O'Neil, about his brother's death. Death, he told her, should be seen as one of the happiest experiences of human life. Miss O'Neil, one of the many people who was healed of an illness through the prayers of Father Solanus, considered what the old Capuchin had just told her. Nevertheless, she was grateful to him for having asked God to cure her.

In February, all the men at St. Felix listened for the news about Cardinal Jozsef Mindszenty, the primate of Hungary. Cardinal Mindszenty had been charged with treason and put on trial by the Communist government in Budapest. The fifty-six-year-old pastor of the Church in Hungary was convicted and sentenced to life in prison. Solanus found the proceedings and the outcome a horrendous injustice and a commentary on the fruits of an atheistic government.[18]

In late April of 1949, Father Solanus and Fathers Ambrose, Angelus, and Herbert from St. Felix set out for Milwaukee by car. They were headed for the unveiling of a statue of a Capuchin, Father Stephen Eckert, who had died there in 1923. Solanus had known him in Yonkers at Sacred Heart, in 1904. He had been so impressed with the holiness of Father Stephen that he worked with others to promote Father Stephen's cause for beatification.

On the way up to Milwaukee, Father Solanus suggested that they stop in Chicago to see his friends the O'Donnells. He assured the other friars that it would be no problem for the O'Donnells to give them a bit of dinner. The other three weren't prepared for the lavish "spread" and the deference they received in a rather grand setting. Father Ambrose De Groot told of the incident years later:

"It turned out they were wealthy people who lived in one of the high-rise apartments along Lake Shore Drive. We found ourselves ushered into a beautifully furnished apartment overlooking Lake Michigan, many stories [up] from the ground level.

"I personally felt embarrassed, calling on these people unannounced, and expecting an invitation to supper. I was rather

172

amazed to see these people brighten up when they saw Father Solanus. They felt sincerely honored and just could not do enough for us. They called a caterer and had a beautiful dinner sent to the apartment. It was borrowed glory as far as I and the rest of us were concerned. It was Father Solanus all the way — the wealthy couple just hung on his words. . . . Father Solanus took it all in stride and just did not notice the fuss made over him. To him these were simply good people who had told him that he would always be welcome in their home."[19]

Another meal which the four friars ate a few days later in Milwaukee was also memorable, but certainly not in the same way. Solanus almost died as a result of it.

At St. Benedict's, where the statue of Father Stephen was dedicated, a ham dinner was served. Solanus was allergic to ham and seldom ate any of it. Because of the occasion, he decided to try a little. This ham, however, was spoiled. A large number of people became ill with food poisoning. Having a more violent reaction to it than others, Solanus had to be rushed to St. Michael's Hospital where he was in serious condition for a while.

Though the four returned to St. Felix Friary in Huntington on April 29, Solanus was still not feeling well. The eczema condition on his legs became acute once more. The friars noticed that something was wrong with his legs again. Solanus was walking instead of running up the stairs.

On May 6, Father Solanus had to be hospitalized at St. Joseph's Hospital in Fort Wayne. His doctors had diagnosed the condition as "weeping eczema," and when the disease was at its worst, the legs of the former porter were covered with painful open sores. The doctors told Father Solanus that they might have to amputate his legs this time. There was very little circulation in the raw, inflamed legs. Father Blase, Solanus's secretary, came to see him and found that the threat of amputation wasn't really preoccupying Solanus. Visitors were!

"It was decided by the friars that word of his hospitalization would not be mentioned. We knew he was seriously ill, and we wanted him to get some rest. To my utter surprise, despite a big 'DO NOT DISTURB' sign on the door, I found fifteen people in the room the next day when I visited him. Some had come from as far away as Detroit. How they found him, I'll never know. But here he was, propped up in bed, with a white canopy over his legs, amiably chatting with his visitors. And sure enough, every three minutes, a disapproving nurse came in to check the pulse in his legs.

"His attitude toward his illness was one of such lack of concern, that I was curious whether he knew how seriously ill he had been and brought up the subject on the way home from the hospital. Yes, he knew that his legs might have to be amputated, but he had the attitude: 'If they came off, it was alright; if not, that was alright too.' "[20]

Solanus remained in Fort Wayne in the hospital until May 22. Warm weather and the prospect of another season as assistant beekeeper and senior gardener may have speeded his recovery. In one part of the garden at St. Felix, Solanus had also been cultivating a patch of wild strawberries which he told the friars he was "taming." After eating them, the friars agreed that the "taming" was worthwhile. The berries were delicious!

By the summer of 1949, Father Solanus had been stationed at Huntington for a little over three years. It was enough time for his many friends to discover just how many miles Huntington was from Detroit or from Chicago or even from Yonkers, New York.

The Capuchin strategy of sending Solanus to an out-of-the-way location had been only partially successful. People in chartered buses came down from Detroit to see Solanus, especially during the summer months. The celebration of Corpus Christi and the name day of Father Solanus (St. Francis Solano on July 21) provided other reasons for the caravans of his friends. St. Felix would host the visitors to Mass (including a Solanus *ferverino*) and then some light refreshment. Then the busloads full of people would reboard the buses and start the five- to six-hour trip home.

Huntington, a small town of about fifteen thousand, also

sensed that there was something unusual, something special, about one of the priests at the friary. And so did the sisters at Victory Noll.

"At Victory Noll, we used to get so many calls and visitors even in the middle of the night," recalled a Victory Noll nun. "People from Chicago or Detroit, from all around the country would come to us, mistaking Victory Noll for St. Felix Friary where Father Solanus lived." Eventually, she said, the local cabdrivers caught on to the confusion outsiders often had. They'd cut right through the muddle over Victory Noll and St. Felix and ask their fares: "Do you want to go to the Victory Noll for men or for women?"[21]

Throughout the remainder of 1949 and into 1950, Father Solanus coped with his workload as best he could. He was nearing eighty and his skin condition and varicose veins made it increasingly difficult to stay as active as he wanted to be. He had always been an advocate of "keeping in trim," as he put it, and being careful about his diet.

Eating fresh vegetables and fruits was necessary to stay in good shape, Solanus often reminded the other friars and the novices at St. Felix. Many of them were city boys and not so enthused about the dietary philosophies of Father Solanus. One "home remedy" for which he found no support at all was walking barefoot in the friary yard, even during cold weather. He believed it stimulated the circulation in his problem legs.

When he was able, he would play volleyball or tennis with the novices. And when he played, he played with total enthusiasm and no holding back. When he fell down, he would pick himself up and continue. If Solanus had any favorite indoor pastime, it was billiards or pool. When no phone calls or visitors interrupted the game, he played with surprising intensity, one of his partners discovered. And he was good!

"He was sly and beat me most of the time," confessed Monsignor James Conroy, who served as chaplain for the Victory Noll Sisters and was a columnist for *Our Sunday Visitor*, the national Catholic newspaper based in Huntington. "You couldn't talk to him at all while you were playing; he had no mercy." Monsignor Conroy (then Father Conroy) discovered that his billiards partner had a "keen sense of humor. Humorous situations never got by him. But he was the soul of humility. I think he would only do what he was directed to do."

From his vantage point, as a priest outside of the Capuchin order, Father Conroy observed that Solanus was treated just as all the other friars, despite his reputation. "I don't think the Capuchins were too impressed with him. Solanus didn't seem to stand out to that extent. He was as familiar as an old shoe."[22]

Others in Huntington also saw Father Solanus in this light. He was clearly a prayerful man who was very close to God. Nevertheless, this smiling blue-eyed man also liked to putter in the garden, loved his Detroit Tigers, and liked to win at billiards, too. He was an approachable holy man.

The young sisters at the Victory Noll novitiate had come to see Father Solanus in this way, too. Victory Noll superiors wanted their nuns to have some contact with this aging man of God. Because of the limitation of his faculties, however, Father Solanus could not serve as any sort of chaplain or confessor at the convent. Instead, in the early 1950s, he was invited regularly to give devotional talks to all the sisters. They would gather in a large hall where the young postulants were seated in front.

Father Solanus would almost always talk about the love of God. At some point during his talk, Solanus would become so absorbed in his topic that he would stop talking. Emotionally moved by the subject, his eyes would fill. At that moment, Solanus would feel the need to pull a large bright blue handkerchief from his Capuchin habit to dab at his eyes.

To the young nuns sitting right in front of him, the gesture had a Charlie Chaplin sort of flourish. The giggling bubbled up and down the row. But the postulants were petrified, thinking of the possible consequences of laughing at such a devout priest. The pause, the handkerchief flourish, the outbreak of chuckling among the postulants, and then the panic were repeated again and again.[23]

Solanus would have reassured the young women had he noticed their discomfort. In his later years, he found more and more joy in young people. And Solanus had always relished contact with children.

In the late 1940s and early 1950s, boxes and boxes of candy began to arrive at St. Felix. They were addressed to Father Solanus, but they were sent by friends who knew he loved to give it to visiting children. Though he knew why the candy had been sent, Father Solanus did not presume to "claim" it for that purpose. He had spent too many years genuinely vowed to poverty and to obedience. The candy was always handed over to Father Guardian each year with no suggestion offered as to its use. The guardian had it all shelved in the friary pantry.

When he wanted to have a little candy to give away, Father Solanus would quietly approach the guardian and ask for some. It was several years before this little mystery was understood by the house superior. The candy Father Solanus requested and carried away by the pocketful was really intended for his own use and distribution.[24]

In June of 1950, Father Solanus was again hospitalized in nearby Fort Wayne. His legs had become covered once again with sores and were hurting terribly. Two weeks later, the legs were again sufficiently healed to release him. Two-week hospitalizations were very difficult for Father Solanus. It wasn't that he was a cranky patient. Solanus was thinking of the stacks of correspondence waiting for him at St. Felix. He also worried just a bit about his gardening enterprises and his beehives.

One of the letters started, but not mailed before his June illness, was one to his sister Margaret and her husband, Frank LeDoux. They had wired about the death of their son Edwin in California. Edwin had apparently been ill for some time. The message Solanus was sending was his predictable blend of sympathy mixed with a spiritual realism about their loss.

"I received your telegram of poor, long-suffering little Edwin. Confident that his was a happy transition rather than a death in the usual sense, I rather congratulate you on having such a chosen one to give to God. . . . Of course I nevertheless sympathize with you on the temporal loss and separation you must for some time expect to experience in this regard."[25]

Somehow, however, the note of condolence was lost for months and Solanus rediscovered it the week before Christmas. He merely continued it and sent it out with a suggestion that "I hope its [sic] better I send it just as it is than start another at this pressing season and as before miss-out [sic] again. . . ." Somehow, Solanus knew that Margaret and Frank would forgive the weaknesses of a brother who'd marked his eightieth birthday the month before.

After he was "liberated" from the hospital on June 30, Solanus was back at it all. Working with the bees with Father Elmer Stoffel, Solanus enjoyed the little creatures he admired so much. According to Father Elmer, Father Solanus often tried "soothing them by playing the harmonica."

Suddenly, three bees stung Father Elmer in quick succession. He fell to the ground, wincing with pain. The assistant beekeeper, Solanus, stood quietly over him and blessed Father Elmer. Immediately, according to Father Elmer, the pain of the stings left him and he had no recurrence of swelling or discomfort.

More and more, Father Solanus was to be found late at night in the chapel. There, he was happily lost in prayer and even, by some accounts, oblivious to outside stimuli. Benedict Groeschel, who was then at the novitiate, saw an example of this sort of prayer by Solanus during the summer of 1950.

"It was a very hot night and I was unable to sleep. About three o'clock in the morning I decided to walk around the cloister a few times and came to the side door leading into the friars' chapel. After a few moments kneeling in the dark, I became aware that someone else was in the chapel quite close to me. Slightly startled, I reached over and put on the spotlight which flooded the sanctuary with bright lights. About ten feet in front of me, kneeling on the top step of the altar with his arms extended in an attitude of profound prayer was Fr. Solanus. He appeared to be totally unaware that the lights had

178

gone on, although his eyes were partly opened and he was gazing in the most intense way at the tabernacle on the altar.''[26]

Father Solanus never moved, Father Benedict Groeschel commented. After a few minutes, feeling like an intruder in something very private and very holy, the young man switched off the light and left the chapel to Father Solanus.

As 1950 drew to a close, Father Solanus received an early birthday present which gladdened his heart as no other gift could. On November 1, Pope Pius XII proclaimed the dogma of the Assumption of the Blessed Virgin Mary. The lifelong devotion Solanus had to the Mother of the Lord seemed to receive a confirmation which he found too joyous for words. In his heart, he'd always known that Mary was in heaven body and spirit.

If anything, the coming and going to and from St. Felix Friary increased throughout the early 1950s. There were more and more individual visitors as well as busloads of visitors coming to talk with Father Solanus. But the friars themselves were also traveling more. The postwar economic boom in this Eisenhower era was making cars more accessible and travel less expensive. The standard of living was swinging upward.

Solanus himself also traveled when he was well. One day, in the parking lot in front of St. Felix he agreed to a quick driving lesson from a local man. The lesson was quickly concluded when his sandal caught in the accelerator pedal, giving Solanus and his Huntington ''instructor'' a few heart-throbbing seconds of concern.

He never learned to drive but always managed to find a ride when he needed one. There were still many friends who provided reason enough to travel back to Detroit. In addition, there were also celebrations, jubilees, and funerals that he wanted to attend. And there were certain culinary delights that seemed to be a Detroit attraction for Solanus.

''He would telephone my sister telling her he was on his way to St. Bonaventure's Monastery in Detroit, having come from Huntington,'' recalls Father Michael Cefai. He was the Detroit pastor at whose parish Solanus had served at weekend Masses, from 1938 to 1945. ''As simply as a child he would ask her if he could have some of her spaghetti on the way. He liked a glass of wine. He also liked Maltese cheese cakes."[27]

Another trip to Detroit, made in December of 1952, had also been preceded by a phone call from Father Solanus. He had called his friend Jerry McCarthy, who was, as the St. Felix Friary Chronicle pointed out, "owner of the largest Chevrolet agency in Detroit, and a very great admirer of Fr. Solanus."[28] Father Guardian had decided that the friary's old car, which had fifty-three thousand miles on it, needed to be traded.

Once the decision was made, Father Solanus humbly reported that he was confident that Jerry McCarthy would give the Capuchins an even trade for a new vehicle! Several days later, Father Guardian, Father Solanus, and another friar drove up the St. Felix Friary drive in a 1952 four-door Chevrolet sedan. It was shining proof that the predictions of Father Solanus were as reliable as ever.

In August of 1952, thirty-seven-year-old Mercedes Ufheil of Huntington went out to see Father Solanus with her parents, Mr. and Mrs. Herman Ufheil. The three were concerned about family illnesses and enrolled their family in the Seraphic Mass Association. Father Solanus spoke to them for about one hour, Mercedes reported. He spoke of the healings he had seen occurring over the years through prayer.

"As we got up to leave, Father Solanus said, 'Little Mary Ann will be well,'" Mercedes said. Mary Ann was suffering from polio and did begin to improve at this time. Solanus made no mention of improving health for Wilfred Ufheil, Jr., who had suffered a birth injury.[29]

In April of 1953, Grace Brady, the sixty-eight-year-old younger sister of Father Solanus died in San Francisco following an illness. It was this sister that Solanus, as a young man, was holding when a horse had thrown them both. He had held on to little Grace with one arm and braced his fall with the other hand. In the process, he broke some finger bones which were not properly set later. It was this Grace who had traveled all the way from the West Coast with Owen in 1947 to share in Solanus's golden jubilee celebration as a Capuchin.

It was also about this time that a young black Capuchin brother named Booker Ashe took over as the secretary for Solanus at St. Felix. Like others before him, Brother Booker simply tried to help the eighty-two-year-old Father Solanus keep up with his correspondence — usually about a hundred to two hundred letters each day. Around holidays, the name day of Father Solanus, or special feasts, the mail would double or triple, he said.

As he always had for other secretaries, Father Solanus would draft replies to people with "pathetic" problems, as he called them. Otherwise, according to Brother Booker, there were only a few directions to "tell Mrs. so and so that she doesn't have to worry about that. She doesn't have to see the doctor again," etc. Handling replies was a large job, too, Brother Booker recalled. For a while, he kept a special file of some of those incoming letters, from 1953-1956.

"I would say that during the time I worked for Father Solanus there must have been five or six hundred such letters from people who were helped through his words of encouragement, through his prayers and so on."[30]

In June of 1953, Father Solanus traveled to Milwaukee to testify in the beatification cause of Father Stephen Eckert. As the summer and autumn months went by, Brother Booker began to fill in as a driver for Father Solanus. On longer drives, Father Solanus invariably talked about "St. Francis in Jesus" and suggested that they say the Rosary and often several Rosaries. Apparently, the recitation of the Rosary was something Solanus nearly always suggested while traveling by car. Brother Booker soon noticed that some of the Capuchins teased Father Solanus about his love of this devotion.

When Solanus was late for meals, Booker remembered, "one of the Fathers would say, 'For your penance for being late, we will *not* say the Rosary next time we drive in the car.'" Solanus accepted the jest without comment and would often say the Rosary on his own when riding in the car with some friars.[31]

Every friar at St. Felix, however, was very much aware

that Father Solanus was only devoted to the Blessed Mother because she was the Mother of the Savior he loved so deeply. He was delighted that Pope Pius XII had declared a Marian Year of devotions which opened on December 8, 1953.

In February of 1954, Father Damasus Wickland, who was almost ninety, was anointed by Father Guardian at St. Felix. Damasus had been a classmate of Father Solanus and was ordained in the same year and with the same faculty limitations as Father Solanus. During his last years, Solanus had often gone to visit him during his free moments. Solanus would read the Little Office of the Blessed Virgin to his ailing classmate who was going blind. On the seventeenth of February, Father Damasus died quietly, leaving Solanus as the only living priest ordained with the Capuchin class of 1904. Solanus had hoped that Damasus would live to mark the golden jubilee of their ordination to the priesthood in July.

In April of 1954, Father Solanus received a phone call from Mrs. Rita Evison of Gaylord, Michigan. Considering the number of calls Solanus got each day, this was just one among the dozens that reached him in a week's time. But Mrs. Evison later believed that the conversation with Solanus was literally lifesaving for her three-month-old baby, Cynthia. Doctors had just told the Evisons that the baby had a heart condition which they believed would kill her.

"I placed a call for Father Solanus," Mrs. Evison reported years later. "At first he could not be located. The telephone operator, who knew I was crying, cut in when the brother said he would look for Father Solanus. The operator said she had heard of Father Solanus and said, 'I'm sure he will help you.'

"When Father Solanus answered, I told him of the extremity. His reply was, 'You're going to bring your baby home in a very few days. I'll go down to the chapel now and I'll pray for her.' "

The next morning, according to Mrs. Evison, the doctor went into the nursery to examine the infant and cried out. A nurse, thinking he'd found the baby dead, rushed to his side. On listening to the baby's heart, the physician had found that the little heart was now beating normally. There were no signs of the irregularity and erratic rhythm which had threatened her life. He had no explanation for the sudden change in a condition which had obviously been congenital. Baby Cynthia did well after that and grew up healthy and strong.[32]

It was a story that now sounded almost routine to the men at St. Felix. They heard so many things about the gifts, the prayers, of Father Solanus. And yet, he was a man who lived among them as one of them. "He was so unassuming that we took everything for granted," explained a Capuchin who'd known Solanus years before in Detroit.

The Capuchins knew the day-to-day Solanus fairly well. They knew of his holiness, but they also knew they couldn't abide his fiddle-playing. They found, too, that he'd begun to "misplace" pies and cakes which devoted local Third Order women constantly bestowed upon him. Solanus would thank the ladies with the greatest sincerity. After they left, however, the aging Solanus, faced with the inevitable stack of correspondence, would push a few books out of the way and shelve the baked goods, meaning to take them to the kitchen later on. But he'd forget! The stale "goodies" would be found later — sometimes weeks later — when a certain book or box of papers was needed off the shelf.

In July of 1954, however, the Capuchins began to turn their attention to Father Solanus and two other priests in a special way. Father Solanus was to get the principal spotlight. He was the only man in the order celebrating a golden jubilee of ordination that year. He was only too happy to share the focus with Father Thomas Aquinas Heidenreich (the Capuchin guardian) and Father Cuthbert Gumbinger. They were both silver jubilarians.

The jubilee Mass was held in St. Mary's Church, Huntington, on July 28. Solanus's brother Monsignor Edward Casey also came to celebrate the occasion. It was a scorching July day, but that didn't discourage the crowds that reassembled after Mass in the larger church hall at the town's other parish, SS. Peter and Paul. At the end of dinner and talks, Father

Solanus concluded with a few short remarks about gratitude to God.[33]

There were many listening to his remarks who had the feeling they'd heard him say the very same words dozens of times before. Father Solanus had no plans to try to impress with his "sermonizing" anyway. By this point, his listeners — in and out of the Capuchin order — knew that the real sermon of this priest's life wasn't what he said. It was the way he believed and loved.

After the buses left and the Huntington excitement quieted down, Father Solanus returned to his daily regimen. As always, it was prayer, letters, phone calls, visitors, community life, outdoor activities, exercise, and then more prayer.

In early November, the St. Felix Friary Chronicle noted, Father Solanus was slowed down with a cold. But the bed rest was only temporary and his health and schedule remained stable throughout winter and into the spring of 1955.

One of the calls received one day in 1955 was from a man named Frank Brady, of Huntington Woods, Michigan. Brady had never met Father Solanus but had heard about him. He was calling about his wife, Katherine, who was lying in a hospital bed scheduled for very dangerous surgery. As Brady later told Father Solanus, Kate had suffered whiplash injury to her neck as a youngster, and the condition had developed into degenerative arthritis.

By this point, she was in constant pain, but doctors had admitted to Frank Brady that surgery could easily kill his wife and the mother of their four children. As Brady detailed the reasons that the doctors wanted to perform the surgery, Father Solanus suddenly interrupted him.

"Oh, no, she won't have the operation," Father Solanus said. "She'll be out in a few days. She'll be back with those children. Now, tell me, how are the Tigers doing?"

Brady may have been too preoccupied to be able to report on the Detroit Tigers, but he soon reported about his wife's recovery to all their friends. One nurse he talked to later called Solanus about her own mother. But she received a different

184

sort of response. "Your mother is quite old," Father Solanus said gently. "God wants her." The mother of the nurse died two days later, but her daughter was resigned to her loss, seeing it as God's will.[34]

Throughout the remainder of 1955, however, the health of Father Solanus became more uncertain. He fell victim to colds and flu more often. His legs ached from the varicose vein problem he'd had for many years. And fellow friars could see that his eyesight was failing rather quickly.

In June of 1955, Father Clement Neubauer became the newly named guardian at St. Felix. He realized immediately that he would have to watch over the failing Father Solanus very carefully. On July 21, the name day of Father Solanus, Father Guardian took special note of the contributions Father Solanus had made as "Director of the Seraphic Mass Association" at the friary.

"Although [almost] 85, Father Solanus is still busy as ever, consoling all the people that come to him," the chronicle reported for that name-day entry, July 21. "Despite the fact that he receives many calls every day, he is a model to all in his faithfulness to religious exercises. His favorite pastime is killing the weeds on the lawn and of course, he is never without his gracious smile."[35]

In November, the friars watched with great interest as their chapel was refurnished and a new altar and platform were put into place. Much of the work was donated by friends of Father Solanus who'd given money for his golden jubilee the year before.

Late in November, a few days before his eighty-fifth birthday, Father Solanus learned of the death of his seventy-four-year-old brother Owen in Seattle. Owen had been the youngest of the Casey boys. Several years earlier, Owen had come to celebrate Christmas with Father Solanus and the St. Felix Capuchins. As December neared, Father Solanus began to experience much greater difficulties with his legs.

CHAPTER ELEVEN

The Doorkeeper Heads Home (1956-1957)

The first several days of 1956 were exceedingly painful for Father Solanus. His skin disease was recurring with a vengeance and he seemed to find no relief from treatments he'd been receiving through his doctors in Fort Wayne.

On January 2, he coped with the pain long enough to participate in the planning of an amateur entertainment program for the St. Felix community.[1] The friars put on the program the following evening. Solanus, of course, played his violin for his part in it. Nonetheless, his brother Capuchins could now catch glimpses of him wincing with pain when he thought he was unobserved. This was a new development. Before, the friars could only guess at his discomfort.

Erysipelas, also known as St. Anthony's fire, is an acute infectious disease of the skin or mucous membranes caused by a streptococcus and characterized by local inflammation and fever. For years, Father Solanus had been combating that and

186

eczema, a skin disease characterized by scaling and itching of the skin. The condition never really left him but was more troublesome for him at various times. The winter of 1955-1956 was one of those periods of more difficulty, and Father Guardian had come to the end of his resources. He had no further ideas about how to help his eighty-five-year-old retired doorkeeper.

After a few phone conversations with Capuchin superiors at St. Bonaventure Friary in Detroit, it was decided to send Father Solanus there. Perhaps in the larger metropolitan area of Detroit, a greater range of medical specialists might produce someone who could do more for Father Solanus.

"Fr. Solanus left for Detroit today, accompanied by Bro. Gabriel," the St. Felix Friary Chronicle reported on January 12. "Father will undergo an examination at one of the hospitals there."[2]

If the Huntington friary report seemed quiet and understated, the news of his arrival in Detroit was guarded with extraordinary secrecy. The sick man was hospitalized for tests, but all the other Capuchins were asked by the guardian of St. Bonaventure, Father Bernard Burke, to say nothing of his presence in the city.[3]

Tests indicated that Solanus had some skin cancers on his legs. An operation was scheduled and performed. Doctors then told the Capuchins that Father Solanus was in relatively good condition for a man of his age and who suffered from the other skin ailments. They admitted that they could not cure the other diseases.

The report on Father Solanus was a pretty encouraging one. As if to reinforce his doctors' prognosis, Solanus improved fairly quickly and was released to return to St. Bonaventure. Once in the house, Father Guardian repeated his order to his friars not to discuss the presence of Father Solanus in their house. Putting Father Solanus under the same obedience, Father Bernard ordered him not to accept calls or visitors without permission — to save his strength.[4] It had already been decided not to send him back to St. Felix for a while.

Solanus gradually improved in this protective environment. His strength returned and he regained some mobility. Walking no longer made his legs, his "faithful sentinels" as he called them, scream with pain. He began to move around again, but only inside the monastery. As far as the rest of the city was concerned, Solanus was still in Huntington, two hundred miles and a long-distance phone call away.

On February 15, Father Solanus received the word that his brother Patrick had died that day in Seattle at the age of eighty-four. Father Solanus took this death hard. Pat had been just one and one-half years younger than Barney. As boys, they were as close emotionally as they were in age. Patrick's death came less than three months after Owen's death. Solanus was experiencing the grief of outliving so many of the brothers and sisters he'd loved so dearly. Only three other Caseys besides himself were still living — Edward, Margaret, and Genevieve.

Though he began to pick up some of his correspondence load once again, Solanus found himself with more time on his hands. When he was feeling well, he spent his hours in the chapel. If he could not meet with people, he could at least pray for them. And as he always had, Solanus prayed with an intensity that his Capuchin brothers found remarkable. The clerical novices, those preparing for the priesthood, occasionally submitted the praying Father Solanus to their own "distraction test." Years before, the cleric novitiate and the brothers novitiate had been separated and the would-be priests were now living at St. Bonaventure.[5]

"On their way to their place in chapel a novice would deliberately detour to walk directly in front of Fr. Solanus," explained Father Dan Crosby who was then one of those novices. "Other novices would have previously been alerted to the test being conducted. Kneeling in their place they would watch to see if Solanus' eyes would open or at least flutter because of the distraction. To their amazement no change was ever registered. Solanus always passed the test."[6]

If Solanus was passing the test young novices were putting him to with flying colors, some of the other friars found him less convincing. On May 10, with no fanfare or announcement of any kind, Father Solanus had been transferred permanently to St. Bonaventure from St. Felix Friary. It was clear that Solanus would be a part of the community at St. Bonaventure for as long as he lived.

At dinner at St. Bonaventure, Solanus began to sit at table between Fathers Elmer Stoffel and Lawrence Merten. Seating was a matter of seniority in religious life, and with almost sixty years of life as a Capuchin, Solanus found himself seated between the master of novices, Father Elmer, and the vicar, Father Lawrence.

Some of the novices had occasionally come to Solanus for advice. The master of novices was not happy with what he'd heard of that advice. Despite the years spent together in Huntington and despite the bee sting healing he'd experienced through Solanus, Father Elmer distrusted Father Solanus.

During the suppers for which no spiritual reading was scheduled and conversation was permitted, Father Elmer often took Father Solanus to task.

"Are you trying to be a saint?" Elmer challenged Solanus, looking at the meager portions Solanus sometimes gave himself. But it was the role the aged doorkeeper was playing with the Seraphic Mass Association that apparently most irritated the master of novices. Over the soup, bread, and vegetables, and with Father Lawrence and others listening in, he jokingly told Solanus his own opinions about his "sanctity" and reputation for holiness. Elmer was convinced that Solanus was grandstanding.

"You're trying to work miracles and taking the honor of them while the Seraphic Mass Association is doing the work," Father Elmer told Solanus more than once. The tone, according to Father Lawrence, was on the lighthearted side, as though one golfer had caught another in trying to fudge on a score.

". . . Father Solanus just looked down and continued eating. He would never in any way be grieved or get mad," recalled Father Lawrence. "He took it [lying down]. Sometimes he laughed and other times you could see it hurt a little."[7] But Father Elmer was not alone in his view of Father Solanus, according to Father Lawrence. "Other friars kidded him a lot about many things, even [his] mispronouncing [of] a word. Some would say that he was bluffing the people."[8]

Though it galled some and mystified others, in a real way Father Solanus inevitably stood apart from his fellow friars. He tried very hard to draw no special attention to himself. But his unique ministry, which Capuchin superiors had overseen for more than fifty years, had set him apart. The calling had come from a source far beyond the mundane and fallible authority of triennial chapters and from elected superiors.

It was a hard calling to leave behind and Father Solanus knew it. After he had been at St. Bonaventure for some months, the word leaked out. It was impossible to keep Solanus virtually "incognito" in a city where he was so well known. He had to go back and forth to doctors. Before long, people began phoning and ringing the doorbell asking for the aged Capuchin. Screening the requests, Solanus's superiors occasionally said "yes" to visitors. Thirty-minute talks were permitted. When Father Solanus was feeling fairly well, Father Lawrence would take a few visitors to his room.

The pain of obeying Father Guardian's ultimatum about visitors and phone calls was grievous. Solanus obeyed but could not really understand the reason for it. As far as fellow Capuchins knew, he expressed that frustration only once — to Brother Ignatius Milne.

"When they were keeping him more confined, he stopped by my desk one day and said: 'Why don't they let me see the people?' " According to Brother Ignatius the tone and expression seemed to say, "So what if I die in the process? What am I all about?"[9]

But for as long as they could, the superiors of Father Solanus kept the protective prohibition intact. He was not to receive visitors or calls without asking their permission, and then only for a short period of time. But the responsibility of the house superiors was to become a lot more difficult.

The secret about the presence of Father Solanus in Detroit was exposed in early December of 1956. The whole city was able to read about it in the *Detroit News*. The paper essentially made a printed announcement of his return to Mt. Elliott Avenue.

Some weeks before, the paper had talked with the Capuchins about doing a special magazine article about the century of service the Capuchins had given in the United States, Fathers Gregory Haas and John Frey having come to the United States in September of 1856 to establish the Capuchin order. The *Detroit News* article was to look at the one hundred years of service given throughout the area. The Capuchins thought it would be a good idea.

Once during the newspaper's advance work for the story, a photographer had been preparing to take pictures of some of the novices in choir. Suddenly, he spotted the venerable old priest with the long, white beard — a perfect subject for the photo. The photographer went over to Father Solanus Casey.

He asked Father Solanus if he would "pretend" to give a blessing to the novices for the photo. "I will not *pretend* to give a blessing," replied Solanus, suddenly indignant. "If you want a blessing, kneel down and I will give one. But I will not *pretend*!" The photographer got the message but also managed to get a photo of Father Solanus giving a real blessing.[10]

When the paper finally arrived, however, the friars were alarmed to see that Father Solanus seemed to be a substantial part of the story. The house chronicle at 1780 Mt. Elliott Avenue registered the surprise. "The Capuchins of Detroit 'made the papers' today. Father Solanus was spread all over the front cover of the Rotogravure section."[11] Within the article, Father Solanus was the only Capuchin directly quoted.

A reporter had apparently asked him his thoughts about his life as a Capuchin. "It's like starting heaven here on earth," Solanus had replied.[12]

For the balance of December 2, Father Guardian and others hoped that the article would not spark an explosion of questions about Father Solanus. Among themselves, they thought

191

that perhaps many of the people who knew Solanus had died or lost interest in him. It had been ten years since Solanus lived in Detroit.

Early in the morning of Monday, December 3, Father Bernard Burke, the Capuchin guardian, could already see that he'd been wrong. Interest in Father Solanus was anything but cold.

"The Brothers at the front door office desk were suffering a headache from answering the avalanche of phone calls," the chronicle for that date stated. The callers "wanted to know whether Father Solanus was available for consultation and blessings."[13] The answer was a polite but firm "no." Those answering the phone explained that Father Solanus was very old and had been ill. His health was delicate, they explained, and meeting with his visitors would be too taxing.

The friends of Father Solanus seemed to understand and asked simply to have their best wishes given to him. The rash of phone calls leveled off. The weather turned colder and Detroiters abandoned themselves to pre-Christmas business. Before the *Detroit News* article, those few allowed to see Solanus had been permitted to do so only with the understanding that they remain silent about it. By Christmas, Father Solanus felt that though he was still bound by obedience in accepting visits, he was no longer bound to act like a living secret.

On Christmas evening, young Frater Dan Crosby stopped for a moment in the friary chapel adjacent to the larger church. In a moment, the novice heard a familiar squeaking noise. The young man opened the connecting door to the church just a bit. Father Solanus had mounted the steps to the church choir loft. With a few lights behind him, the eighty-six-year-old was in his own world, entertaining the newborn Christ Child. Father Solanus was playing Christmas carols on his violin and singing them softly. It was his own Christmas tradition and he'd kept it up for many years.

As the year drew to a close, Solanus continued to enjoy a period of relatively good health. Though he did not talk about it, it must have been an extremely difficult year for him. For the first time since his assignment to Yonkers as a young priest, he was limited in his contact with people, the ones he'd been ordained to serve.

This was a great hardship for Father Solanus, while some of the smaller pleasures, the pleasures of life in the country in Huntington, were also gone. He could no longer take walks in an orchard or tend to bees. The large vegetable gardens, the vineyard, and the lawns of St. Felix were no longer part of his daily walking tour. He had left the country for the city, and even though it was a city he loved, it was painful. Yet Solanus "thanked God" even for these changes.

In January of 1957, however, many of his fellow friars at St. Bonaventure had begun to think that Father Solanus was right where he should be. When superiors checked their records, they could see that Father Solanus would be marking sixty years in the order on January 14. It seemed right that he should celebrate that occasion in Detroit. He would be able to repeat his vows in the same friary chapel in which he'd said them for the first time.

January fourteenth dawned cold and clear. In the morning, the Capuchins gathered with their jubilarian in the refectory. To forestall the dangers of an overcrowded church, the monastery announced that the occasion would not be open to the public. Nevertheless, a few laymen were already waiting in the larger church when Father Solanus and the friars processed into the sanctuary.

There, Solanus stood and listened to the invocation of Father Bernard Burke, the guardian. He was only a few feet from the spot where he'd been kneeling when, at the age of twenty-six, he had entered Capuchin life on January 14, 1897.

Finally, Solanus was given a sheet of paper on which was written the vows which he was to repeat. This act formally recommitted him to religious life and to his vows of poverty, chastity, and obedience. But Father Solanus had apparently been thinking of his life which he understood was almost over. It was really God *and* his Capuchin superiors who were to receive this renewed gift of his life, the life that was left. The thought of it all and of the mercy of God made the deep-set blue eyes fill with tears.

Solanus had to stop reading several times. Everyone in the chapel knew that Solanus had been suffering with more eye trouble in recent years. This time, however, the difficulty was a matter of emotions rather than aging eyes. As he continued to read in his high-pitched voice his eyes finally overflowed and he couldn't continue to speak. Father Giles Soyka was standing nearby. Giles reached over, gently took the copy of the vows from the hands of Solanus, and finished reading them for him.[14]

But Solanus was probably not the only man in the chapel who felt the emotion of the moment welling up inside. It was unreasonable to think that Father Solanus would have many more occasions to repeat his vows of Capuchin commitment.

In February and in March, however, Father Solanus remained relatively healthy. The skin ailments were under control. On St. Patrick's Day, March 17, he wrote cheerfully to his only living brother, Monsignor Edward. He tucked twenty dollars into the letter, telling Ed that the money was for his fund-raising efforts for the missions in the Philippines.[15]

During Lent, Solanus was getting around fairly well and he had time to serve in little ways. He was feeling sufficiently mobile one day to serve as "altar boy" for a visiting priest, Father Michael Dalton. Father Michael hadn't really met the elderly friar who materialized from somewhere in the chapel to serve his Mass. Father Michael was nonetheless very impressed when Solanus knelt and kissed the floor in front of the tabernacle as he passed it. It was a gesture St. Francis had urged his Friars Minor to repeat many centuries earlier.

After the Mass, the devout friar whom Father Michael had assumed to be a brother took him to breakfast and introduced himself as "Father Solanus." Something about this elderly man profoundly touched the visitor. He asked Solanus to hear his confession. "I'm only a simplex priest — no faculties to absolve," Solanus replied to the startled Father Dalton.[16] After Solanus told more about his ministry, Father Michael could see that the faculties God had given to this aged acolyte were really remarkable.

While Father Michael unexpectedly "discovered" Father Solanus in the role of "oldest altar boy," a few visitors and callers had contact with him in unusual circumstances.

Mrs. Mary Klimczak phoned St. Bonaventure's Monastery in March. Not really expecting to have the chance to talk with Father Solanus, she asked if she could leave a message for him. Her overburdened mother was very disturbed emotionally and at the point of despair. The brother or priest who answered the phone left for a moment to relay the message.

Suddenly, a high-pitched voice was on the phone — "Father Solanus speaking." Overwhelmed at first, Mrs. Klimczak regained her composure and began to tell Solanus of her problem. After asking for a few details, Father Solanus urged her to read one volume of *The Mystical City of God* by Mother Mary Agreda. He also advised that she try to receive Holy Communion more often.

Mary Klimczak readily agreed to it all and listened very carefully. As the conversation was drawing to a close Father Solanus paused and then assured her that "things will change today. Come to see me." Time proved Father Solanus right, this caller discovered.

Not many callers or visitors had this kind of access to the weakening Father Solanus during the early spring. By May, the skin eruptions that had obliged him to go back to Detroit forced his return to St. John's Hospital. Capuchin superiors and Brother Gabriel, a lay brother who had been caring for Father Solanus, were pulled aside. Doctors confided that the patient might die at any moment.

The condition of Father Solanus deteriorated dramatically. His physicians did not seem to know how to stem the inflammation. An oxygen tent was ordered to help him breathe. Not long after the tent was in place, the patient began to rally. In fact, to the surprise of Brother Gabriel and the medical staff surrounding him, Solanus began to breathe with some regained strength. Then he began to sing his favorite Marian hymns!

One verse. Then a second verse through. When Father Solanus sang straight through a third verse and began a fourth, Brother Gabriel could stand it no longer. He was terrified that Solanus might use his last breath just to sing. He begged Solanus to stop singing and save his strength. Immediately, Father Solanus became very quiet and offered no word of protest.[17]

As the days went by, the patient grew a little stronger. Hearing that Father Solanus was improving, many people found their own ways of having some contact with him.

"How about a blessing, Father?" requested Sister Arthur Ann, a nurse.

"All right," quipped Solanus, "I'll take one!" But Solanus did not refuse her a blessing or a request she made of him later. Seeing him prepare to say the Rosary in the chapel one day, Sister Arthur Ann impulsively pulled out her own rosary and asked the priest to use hers. She wanted to have it as a keepsake later on, she explained. Father Solanus reluctantly agreed and laid his own rosary beads in his lap.[18]

When Father Solanus felt well enough, he was wheeled down to St. John's chapel. There he would say Mass or his office or Rosary. He often asked that others read to him there from his favorite devotional work, *The Mystical City of God*. Somehow, word got around whenever Solanus was making his way to or from chapel. Patients, their families, and hospital staffers would line the hallway, asking Father Solanus to bless them. He never failed to do so, but he constantly tried to downplay his role as the medium of those blessings.

". . . I have so often heard people speak of you," commented Sister Arthur Ann one day.

"Yes, people often speak of Jesse James too," he retorted with a laugh.[19]

Day by day throughout late May, Father Solanus improved and was finally able to leave the hospital for St. Bonaventure's. However, his days of fair health were very short. On June 14, he was readmitted to St. John's so that his doctors could cope with the resurgence of disease more aggressively. But Solanus was tiring more readily now and losing weight. Shortly after the second return home, he was rushed to the hospital again. And then again.

The house chronicle at St. Bonaventure recorded the date — July 2. The medical staff at St. John's now discovered that the skin inflammation covered the entire body of Father Solanus. That made treatment even more difficult. Intravenous feeding tubes inserted to keep him from becoming dehydrated — and even routine examinations — now caused great pain to the patient because of his red, scaling skin.

Doctors were doing their best to make Father Solanus as comfortable as possible, but there was little that they could do. From their perspective, this old priest was clearly dying, but he would be dying with great pain.

As the July days came and went, Father Solanus lost his appetite and could hardly eat anything. Erysipelas, one of the diseases afflicting him, was known to inflame mucous membranes as well as the skin. Nurses gave him small bits of lemon peel to chew on to slake his thirst.[20]

By this time, Solanus was making no attempt to hide the pain he was suffering. "My whole body hurts, thanks be to God," he admitted. It was very clear to everyone that he was accepting this final and unremitting pain with a Christian joy. Solanus understood very well that he was dying. All of his attention and his mental energy were now focused on salvation — his own and the salvation of others.

Father Gerald Walker, the forty-six-year-old Capuchin provincial, came to see him often during these July days. He told him about the many calls, telegrams, and greetings that were flooding into St. Bonaventure's. The whole city of Detroit was praying for him, the provincial told Solanus.

There was a very special relationship between Solanus and Father Gerald, whom Solanus had first met as a small boy. He had come with his parents to see Father Solanus during the late 1920s. Over the years, Solanus apparently grew to think of Gerald as a spiritual son and Gerald revered Solanus as a father. Since Solanus had come back to Detroit, where Father

Gerald was serving as provincial, the regard and love between them grew even deeper.

"I am offering my sufferings that all might be one," gasped Father Solanus during one visit with Father Gerald. "If I could only live to see the conversion of the whole world. . . ."[21]

In recent years, Father Solanus, always a keen observer of world events, had become increasingly concerned about that "whole world." He was appalled to see the power that an atheistic nation, Soviet Russia, had gained in the postwar world. And in the previous year, Father Solanus had been shocked to read about the crushing of organized religion and freedom in Hungary by a nation that denied the existence of God.

He also shook his head often over what he viewed as a growing American materialism. This concern about consumerism was shared one day while talking with Sister Arthur Ann in his hospital room. "So often people hope to find happiness in money or the things money buys," he told her. "If only they would stop running around, acquiring this or that, instead of seeking happiness only where it can be found — in love of God. They are so foolish."[22] He worried so much about materialism because it jeopardized a sound spirituality.

It was totally in character for Father Solanus to be so concerned about others even while he knew he was dying. He simply could not forget about "the people." Serving those people had been his life's work. He seemed to relish and "thank God" for his suffering in the hope that accepting it would be of service to others.

"I looked on my whole life as giving and I want to give until there is nothing left of me to give," Solanus confided to Father Gerald. Father Gerald looked at the emaciated body of the man he'd grown to love so dearly and could barely keep himself from shouting. Anyone could see that at this point there was very little left of Solanus to give.[23] What he had left to give, however, Solanus was still giving.

Mrs. Gladys Feighan, of Utica, Michigan, was visiting her mother at St. John's Hospital when she overheard that Father

Solanus Casey was also hospitalized there. That was extraordinary good news for her. She had been hoping for several years to ask him to pray for her special intention. When Father Solanus was still stationed in Huntington, she'd passed up a chance to take a chartered bus to see him because she'd discovered she was pregnant.

Mrs. Feighan lost that pregnancy as she had lost two others. She had one living child and longed for another. Because of the Rh factor, doctors advised her that her chances for another baby were very poor indeed. (The Rh factor can bring about erythroblastosis fetalis, or Rh disease, which, in certain cases, may result in death for the infant.)

Hoping against hope that she would get a chance to talk with Father Solanus for a few moments, Gladys Feighan went to the nurses' station on the floor where Father Solanus was. Referred immediately to Brother Gabriel, Mrs. Feighan briefly explained her case. Brother Gabriel left her and went to talk with Father Solanus.

In five minutes, she was being ushered in to see the man she'd heard such wonderful stories about. He was extremely thin and obviously in great pain, but his bright blue eyes and a smile were directed entirely at her. To spare him a long history of her troubles, Mrs. Feighan spoke of her great desire to have another child and of the death of three other children through miscarriage.

"A baby!" Father Solanus marveled, smiling at her. "For a woman to want a baby — how blessed — and then to hold God's own creation in your hands!" Solanus assured her that her desire was not a selfish one but a very normal one, one oriented to "doing God's work" by bringing up a child as he should be brought up. One didn't always meet women who wanted children, he said. Gladys Feighan then confessed her sorrow that her three unborn children had died without the saving grace of baptism.

"That is not for you to concern yourself about," answered Solanus. "Just have confidence in our dear Lord's infinite love." He continued to talk about God's love and his voice began to tremble with emotion. He blessed his visitor and was quiet for a moment.

"You will have another child, Gladys. You must believe this with all your heart and soul," he told her. "You must believe this so strongly that before your baby is born you will get down on your knees and thank the Blessed Mother. Because once you ask her, and thank her, there's nothing she can do but go to her Son and ask Him to grant your prayer."

There were tears in the blue eyes looking at her so intently, Mrs. Feighan said later. She left, touched by the encounter, pondering the unshakable faith she had seen in the eyes of a holy man who was dying. She began to try to live in that faith from that hour. Five years later, as time would tell, she was doubly blessed with the birth of twins — a son and a daughter.[24]

In the last week of July, Monsignor Edward Casey arrived in Detroit, as did Mrs. Martha Casey, the widow of Owen. Both planned to stay at the hospital full time to serve their dying Father Solanus. Martha had been the administrator of a nursing home in Seattle. It was hoped that she could help protect Father Solanus from visitors who were still asking to see Solanus.

Family members had been informed by the Capuchins that their brother and uncle was not expected to survive this bout with his illness. He no longer had the strength to fight the disease successfully.

On July 30, Father Gerald stopped by to see Father Solanus during the evening. He looked weaker than before, Father Gerald thought. But Solanus wanted to talk. Since talking obviously tired him, the provincial tried to slow him down. As Father Gerald prepared to leave, Solanus looked at him intently and said: "Tomorrow will be a wonderful day." The meaning was not lost on Father Gerald. He walked out of the room and out of the hospital with the words echoing inside his head. Father Solanus had predicted the date of his death.[25]

Monsignor Edward had not heard that comment. He rose early on Wednesday, July 31, to say his Mass in the hospital chapel. His special intention was for his ailing brother. Afterward, at about 8:00 A.M., he went to the hospital room to see

Father Solanus. The patient wanted to talk. Like Father Gerald, Edward had trouble keeping Solanus quiet. Solanus spoke of the need for conversion and his longing to evangelize. It was the subject, Edward noted, that always made his brother's eyes glow.

To make sure that Father Solanus would get a bit of morning rest, Monsignor Ed finally left him. Looking back, for a moment, he could see that his brother had a number of covers over him despite the midsummer heat that was already beginning to bake the hospital room. Edward turned and went to his own room to write some letters to relatives about the seeming improvement Father Solanus was now showing.

Just before eleven that morning, an orderly, a nurse, and a maid entered the room of Father Solanus. They were going to change the bed linens and bathe him. The routine task had to be done so delicately for this patient. His raw and inflamed skin made it excruciating to be moved.

It seemed as if Solanus might be dozing, but then they noticed that he was whispering something they could not understand. The orderly supported his head and shoulders as the nurse pulled his hospital gown over his shoulders in order to bathe him. Suddenly, the blue eyes opened wide and Father Solanus stretched out his arms.

"I give my soul to Jesus Christ," he said clearly. The eyes closed and he fell backward a bit, exhaling his last breath. It was just 11:00 A.M.

Just then a couple of the nuns came in and Mother Aileen had Monsignor Edward phoned. Within a minute's time, Edward came down the hall and entered the room to see that his brother was truly gone. After a minute or two, he led a Rosary for Father Solanus but couldn't finish it. Word went out quickly to St. Bonaventure's and then to Capuchin houses where Father Solanus had served or was known. By early evening, thousands in Detroit were in a state of mourning that had no precedent.

Back at the monastery later in the afternoon, it was noted that Father Solanus had died at exactly the hour he had started his first Mass on the same day of July fifty-three years earlier. It had been 11:00 A.M. on July 31, 1904, when a dark-haired, bearded young man ascended to the altar in a little church in Appleton, Wisconsin. The life of Father Solanus had ended with a mysterious and wonderful repetition.

In Huntington, the friar keeping the chronicle thought for a bit and then made his entry concerning the death: "We found out about the death of Father Solanus, but we are happy for him because he wanted to die and go home to God where he can now see Him face to face."[26]

CHAPTER TWELVE

A Legacy
of Faith
and Charity

News of the death of Father Solanus Casey spread quickly
throughout Detroit on July 31. Friends called and consoled one
another. There was the sense among many that they would
never again know anyone like him. In almost every conversation about the porter, the words "charity" and "faith" were
used or implied. The evening news in Detroit broadcast the
city's loss to thousands more who had still not heard of it. The
Detroit News and the *Detroit Free Press* were already preparing their obituary notices with follow-up features planned.

No one, however, anticipated the way Detroit would mourn
this man many called "Father Capuchin."

Soon after his death, the thin and worn body of Father
Solanus was transported to Van Lerberghe Funeral Home on
east Warren Street. The Capuchins were aware that the following of Father Casey was large. Van Lerberghe's offered ample
facilities for a larger wake than could be held at other
mortuaries. Visiting hours, it was announced, would begin at
10:00 A.M. on Thursday, August 1.

203

By 6:30 A.M. on Thursday, crowds of people were already lined up down to the corner in front of Van Lerberghe's on Warren. Just before ten, concerned about the size and potentially excitable state of the crowd, the funeral home director went out to the front and assured everyone that they would be able to see Father Solanus. He asked them to line up in two columns, which were then to pass by the casket on either side.

The people ordered themselves and began to file in and were soon viewing the man they revered so deeply. Father Solanus was dressed in his Capuchin habit with its hood pulled up over his head. A rosary and copies of the Rule and Constitution of the Order had been laid inside the casket near him. Capuchins were posted nearby to prevent any attempts to obtain "relics" from the habit or body. But they were also there to receive the expressions of sympathy and love for their brother.

The "pilgrimage" continued throughout the day and into the evening. By 10:30 P.M., when funeral home assistants closed the doors, more than five thousand people had passed by the remains of Father Solanus Casey. Among the visitors were people of every age, race, and nationality. Many mothers carried their children by to see Father Solanus. Non-Catholics as well as Catholics came.

On the following morning, Friday, August 2, no scheduled visitation was planned. The body of Father Solanus was to be taken to St. Bonaventure's Monastery Chapel for further viewing there. However, by 6:30 A.M., hundreds of people were again gathered in front of Van Lerberghe's. They rang the bell and asked admittance until the casket had to be moved. Arthur Van Lerberghe gave his approval, and the people again moved into the viewing room and past the body of the Capuchin they loved.

The story was the same later in the day at St. Bonaventure's. Hundreds of people stood outside in the August heat in order to get a brief last look at Solanus. By three o'clock that afternoon, six thousand people had come, stopped for a prayerful moment, and then moved out of the monastery chap-

204

el. By Saturday morning, the number of visitors during the wake totaled twenty thousand.[1]

Many who came, stopped to tell the Capuchins that they had experienced healings through Father Solanus. Cancer, polio, deafness, psychotic depression: the "litany" of human hurts that had been healed or accepted through Solanus seemed to be as long as the line of viewers. His brother friars listened with growing amazement. "I can see so very clearly now what I failed to see fully at the time," one Capuchin said later of Solanus.[2] Later, the idea was echoed over and over throughout the province and in the friaries where Father Solanus had tried to live a low-profile holiness.

At the funeral of Father Solanus on Saturday, August 3, his only living brother, Monsignor Edward Casey, was celebrant while Father Gerald Walker, the provincial, gave the homily. Later, Monsignor Edward, speaking to a news reporter, said: Solanus "was a very spirited youngster but was also very pious." All the years of his example contributed to religious vocations in the family, he added. Father Solanus was survived by two sisters and, of course, Monsignor Edward, as well as by many nieces and nephews, including two priests and twelve nuns. "Father Solanus is a family legend as well," commented the younger brother.[3]

But legends have their own proper time for popular recognition. The time for the example of Father Solanus to become even better known had not yet arrived. He was buried in the small graveyard on the end of the block St. Bonaventure Monastery occupied. There were seventeen other friars already there, and the standard gravestone soon indicated that he was not to be singled out from the others.

"Rev. Francis Solanus Casey, O.F.M., Cap. Born Nov. 25, 1870. Ordained July 24, 1904. Died July 31, 1957. Age 86. Religious 60. RIP." It was only in preparing deathcards and the script for the stone that his proper birthday was discovered. For sixty years, Father Solanus had not bothered to "correct" the Capuchin record, which had incorrectly listed his date of birth as October 25 rather than November 25.

In the months following his death, people continued to come to visit the grave. An enclosure surrounding the grave-yard admitted anyone who wished to go in. But inside the friary where he had spent so many years, the few articles he left behind were rather quickly distributed or shelved. For a number of years, it looked as though they would remain shelved.

In 1962, seven old notebooks were found among his effects. They contained short notes that were dated from 1924 to 1956 and soon proved to have been the notebooks of Father Solanus Casey. They were precious notebooks, filled with the rather small tight handwriting of a man who'd been ordered to keep an "account book" on God's "favors." On careful examination of the notebooks, it was noticed that on six hundred to seven hundred of the entries Father Solanus had gone back later to include additional information about healings or the astonishing answers to prayers.

The collecting of other writings and records came later. In 1961, the year before Monsignor Edward Casey died, the last of the Casey sons sat down with author James Derum (*The Porter of Saint Bonaventure*) to share his memories of Father Solanus. In 1972, less than twenty years after his death, the accumulated documentation and memories of Solanus Casey prompted the first official step toward further study of his holiness.

The National Council of Catholic Bishops gave a *nihil obstat* (a statement that "nothing hinders" further investigation). A vice-postulator, Father Paschal Siler, had been appointed to gather information in 1966. Eight years later he was succeeded by Brother Leo Wollenweber. Brother Leo had known Father Solanus but admitted more recently that "now I know him better than I did when he was living." In 1976, the year of the American bicentennial, the vice-postulator gave a formal petition to Detroit's Cardinal John F. Dearden to initiate the cause of beatification and canonization within the archdiocese.

Throughout the late 1970s and 1980s, the investigation of information, correspondence, and records has continued. The official testimony of fifty-three witnesses was taken to Rome from Detroit in October of 1984. The "informative process" was conducted by Archbishop Edmund C. Szoka, who succeeded Cardinal Dearden. The testimonies and all other official records were given to the Sacred Congregation for the Causes of Saints.

In general terms, such an investigation looks for proof that the person practiced virtue to a heroic degree. Study of the character of the person's faith, hope, and love of God and of neighbor is mandated as a component in the investigative process. If the Sacred Congregation for the Causes of Saints should vote favorably on the implications of the official testimonies and other documents, the case is passed on to the pope. If the Holy Father declares that the evidence of "heroic virtue" is certain, he declares the person "venerable."

In the later stages of the process, investigators seek proof of miracles linked to the person. If they can substantiate one, the process can proceed to move the cause toward "beatification." If the person is beatified, it is accomplished in a public ceremony conducted by the pope. If later study surfaces proof of a miracle occurring after the beatification, the process can move toward "canonization."

In July of 1987, another step was taken which was to expedite the investigation of Father Solanus Casey's cause. Shortly after sunrise on July 8, the grave of Solanus in St. Bonaventure Cemetery was opened. Workmen raised the casket buried there almost three decades earlier. It was then carried around the corner and into the church to a room adjoining the chapel.

There, Archbishop Edmund Szoka of Detroit, other Church officials, Capuchin witnesses, two Casey family members, and mortuary authorities gathered to view the body. Dr. Gordon Rose, head of the Department of Mortuary Science at Wayne State University, conducted the examination in the room, which was stifling with July heat. Verification of the identity of the body is a required procedure in the canonization investigation, and when the casket of Father Solanus was opened, the body was readily recognizable to those who had known him or had seen photos of him.

Data for a report on the state of the body was also collected. A report was to be sent on to Rome. The report stated that the structural and tissue integrity of Solanus Casey was extensive. Monsignor Albert Allen, the archbishop's delegate in the canonization cause, added that the remains were "an intact body — however, not perfectly so." Some decomposition in both arms had occurred. The body was then washed, dressed in a fresh habit, and placed into a new bronze-colored steel casket. The casket was sealed and carried in a quiet procession into the chapel, where visitors can more easily view the grave and pay their respects.

"Father Solanus could be the first American-born man canonized," explained Brother Leo Wollenweber.[4] But no predictions of such eventualities can be or need to be made to make the story of Father Solanus any more valuable. It was his goodness that makes his story so relevant and inspirational. His was a very selfless love which so successfully communicated an uncomplicated faith in a loving God.

"He had a sparkle in his eyes and a very delightful sense of humor," remembered Mary Casey Molloy, daughter of Father Solanus's oldest brother, Jim. As a young woman, she had moved to Detroit to work, leaving behind her family in Seattle. During the years she lived and worked in Detroit, the Great Depression was swelling the lines of visitors seeking to see Father Solanus. His workload was increasing. With mixed feelings, Mary would stop in once in a while to see her uncle after work.

"I would take my place with other visitors at the Monastery office sometimes waiting half an hour or more. As he stood up to say good-bye to the person he was speaking with, he might glance up and spot me. Then he would beckon to me to step inside his small inner office. I would feel guilty to thus get ahead of others waiting before me. When he would get a chance to come in and talk to me, he always wanted the news of the family, especially my Dad and Mother. He also asked news of all my Uncles and Aunts in the Casey family.

"Sometimes if I hadn't stopped in to see him for several weeks he would call me by phone. In his wispy voice he would say, 'This is your old Uncle just calling to hear how you are and what's the news from Seattle.' "[5]

Until he headed to his final home, Father Solanus Casey never lost his interest and his joy in the news from home, and the "good news" within people growing in faith and thankfulness to the Father of all. *Deo Gratias* — "Thanks be to God."

WORDS AND WISDOM
OF FATHER SOLANUS
(From His "Collected Writings")

Appreciation • To know is to appreciate. God Himself can be appreciated — and loved — only inasmuch as He is known.

Atheism • Atheism [is] the very climax of intellectual stupidity, or moral insanity, or diabolically devilish perversity. The height of insanity is not to believe in God, for only a fool says in his heart that there is no God when the heavens and the earth proclaim his glory. Atheism robs man of supernatural hope — the very soul of happiness.

Bitterness • We are never justified in being "bitter" toward anyone except ourselves. In very deed, if we were only one tenth as appreciative as we have every reason to be, our gratitude for what God has done for us — directly and through His creatures, most especially through our immediate superiors — would be such that we would be perfectly content with what we are and what we have.

Burdens of Ministry • Sometimes of course it becomes monotonous and extremely boring, till one is nearly collapsing, but in such cases, it helps to remember that even when Jesus was about to fall the third time, he patiently consoled the women folk and children of his persecutors, making no exceptions.

Christian Life • We are Christians only in as far as we believe in Jesus and keep His word.

Conversion • Only in heaven can we be satisfied as being fully and really converted. Pray for the conversion of sinners — including poor Father Solanus.

Crosses • Crosses [are] the best school wherein to learn appreciation for the love of Jesus Crucified. . . . If we only try to show the dear Lord good will and ask him for resignation to the crosses he sends or permits to come our way, we may be sure that sooner or later they will turn out to have been just so many blessings in disguise.

Death • Death is the climax of all humiliation, when we must finally give up all and turn all over to God. Death can be very beautiful — like a wedding — if we make it so.

Distractions in Prayer • Do such distractions displease the Good God? For myself, I do not think that they do. I would answer, as I have occasionally done now and then to assure scrupulous souls: No, Jesus is no crank. He knows that we are not angels, but poor sinners.

The Eucharist • How often I regret that daily Holy Communion was not recommended when we were young. I feel now that we missed so much that would have strengthened us against the dangers and temptations of youth.

God's Grace • Were we only to correspond to God's graces, continually being showered down on everyone of us, we would be able to pass from being great sinners one day to [being] great saints the next. We are continually immersed in God's merciful grace like the air that permeates us.

God's Timing • God, who loves tiny beginnings, will know as He always does know, how and when to provide developments.

Gratitude • Gratitude is the first sign of a thinking, rational creature. Be sure, if the enemy of our souls is pleased at anything in us, it is ingratitude of whatever kind. Why? Ingratitude leads to so many breaks with God and our neighbor.

Holiness • As manifested in the lives of the saints, if we strive and use the means God has given us, we too can ascend to great sanctity and to astonishing familiarity with God, even here as pilgrims to the Beatific Vision.

Hope • Hope — the very soul of happiness — [on] this side of heaven.

Human Community • How merciful is the Good God in making us dependent on one another.

Humility • If you can honestly humble yourself, your victory is won.

Justice • Disregard for the claims of justice, under whatever pretext, has always been a manifestion, to say the very least, of shallow thinking, or rather a betrayal of real thinking. Only lovers of justice and truth can possess the Kingdom of Heaven, and to be children of God we must be lovers of justice, truth, and peace.

Living in the Present • Man's greatness lies in being faithful to the present moment. We must be faithful to the present moment or we will frustrate the plan of God for our lives.

Marriage • Marriage should be held as it ought to be, and is, as something sacred, to be prepared for with purity and holiness of heart and embraced in a Christian manner. Those who embrace it should do so determined to bear the burdens of the holy state they enter. They should remember that their duties and privileges are one and the same and must be taken as such if peace is to reign in the individual soul, in the family, and in human society.

Mary, the Blessed Virgin • Mary is our Mother because she has given Jesus wholly to us, human and divine. There is no one else on earth or in heaven that God Himself loves as He loves His ever Virgin Immaculate Mother and wishes her to be known and loved.

Parenthood • God has given a specially beautiful coloring to the love of those whose privilege it is to have become earnest and faithful parents. To raise children for God and society is manifestly pleasing to God. And this, whether by natural generation or adoption (seemingly quite a matter of indifference to Him).

Peace • Peace is the outstanding characteristic of charity. They accompany each other and must begin if really genuine, between God and the individual soul. For the individual, peace is not possible except in the willing service of his Creator.

Penance • God knows as no one else knows how we all and each need penance. God knows we need humiliations whereby we can foster humility. Hence in His love, He never fails to provide occasions for each one to practice penance.

Providence • God's plans are always for the best: always wonderful. But most especially for the patient and the humble who trust in Him are His plans unfathomably holy and sublime. There is a little verse I am sure will profit you to keep in mind and ought to help you foster confidence in God: "God condescends to use our powers, if we don't spoil His plans by ours."

Reason for Life • Life is to live and life is to give and talents to use for good if you choose. Do not pray for easy lives, pray to be stronger. Do not pray for tasks equal to your powers, pray for powers equal to your task. Then the doing of your work shall be no miracle but you shall be a miracle. Every day you shall wonder at yourself, at the richness of life which has come to you by the grace of God.

Religion • The only science that gives purpose to every other science is the science of Religion. Religion is the science of our happy relationship with and our providential dependence on God and on our neighbor. Religion is the science of saving souls.

Resignation • How wonderful the ways of the Good God — when we foster confidence in Him by just leaving at least something that seems important for Him to take care of.

Sacrifices • Sacrifices willingly made for God's sake are always a small sacrifice for the results sure to follow. Deo Gratias!

Suffering • We do well to remember how short, after all, it is till our suffering and our time of merit will be over. Let us offer everything therefore to the divine Spouse of souls, that we may accept it as helping Him to save immortal souls, our own included.

Thanking God • Let us thank Him at all times and under whatever circumstances. Thank Him for our creation and our existence, thank Him for everything — for His plans in the past that by our sins and our want of appreciation and patience have so often been frustrated and that He so often found necessary to change. Let us thank Him for all His plans for the future — for trials and humiliations for as well as great joy and consolations; for sickness and whatever death He may deign to plan.

Therefore we should thank Him frequently for, not only the blessings of the past and present, but thank Him ahead of time for whatever He foresees is pleasing to Him that we suffer. We should do this not only in general but in each particular case.

Theological Virtues • Like the Holy Trinity, Faith, Hope, and Charity are one. Theoretically, Faith, like the Eternal Father, comes first, but in both cases they are essentially one.

Tolerance • Be as blind to the faults of your neighbor as possible, trying at least to attribute a good intention to their actions.

Trust in God • In my opinion there is hardly anything else that the enemy of our soul [that is, Satan] dreads more than confidence — humble confidence in God. Confidence in God is the very soul of prayer.

Vocational Happiness • We should be grateful for and love the vocation to which God has called us. This applies to every vocation, because after all, what a privilege it is to serve God even in the least capacity.

Weaknesses • The weaknesses we experience are naturally providential guards against one of the very greatest dangers to holiness — pride.

Work of Humanity • In His divine economy, God has honored His creatures — most especially rational ones — by giving them each according to his ability a part of His own work to do — by participation in His own divine activity.

Worry • Shake off excessive worry and exercise a little confidence in God's providence. . . . Last year it was something that you now smile about. Tomorrow it's about something that will not be serious if you raise your heart to God and thank Him for whatever comes. . . . How merciful the Good God is, always fitting the back to the burden if not vice-versa, as often is the case!

CHAPTER NOTES

Chapter 1

1. Joseph P. O'Grady, *How the Irish Became Americans* (Boston: Twayne Publishers, Div. of G.K. Hall & Co., 1973), p. 38.
2. Sister M. Justille McDonald, *History of the Irish in Wisconsin in the Ninteenth Century* (Washington, D.C.: The Catholic University of America Press, 1954), p. 3.
3. Thomas Sowell, *Ethnic America: A History* (New York: Basic Books, Inc., 1981), p. 21.
4. James Patrick Derum, *The Porter of Saint Bonaventure* (Detroit: Fidelity, 1968), p. 29.
5. Ibid, p. 30.
6. Ibid.
7. Sowell, op. cit., p. 25.
8. McDonald, op. cit., p. 8.
9. Jay P. Dolan, *The American Catholic Experience* (Garden City, N.Y.: Doubleday, 1985), p. 137.
10. McDonald, op. cit., p. 288.
11. Howard Mead, Jill Dean, and Susan Smith, *Portrait of the Past: A Photographic Journey Through Wisconsin* (Madison, Wis.: Wisconsin Tales and Trials, 1971), p. 42.
12. Brother Leo Wollenweber, O.F.M. Cap., "Articles of Testimonial Proof . . . of Father Solanus Casey, O.F.M. Cap.," p. 1.
13. Derum, op. cit., p. 23.
14. Solanus Casey, Letter to Msgr. Edward Casey, April 23, 1953, "Collected Writings Attributed to the Servant of God Father Solanus Casey, O.F.M. Cap.," Vol. I, p. 190.
15. Mead et al., op cit., p. 29.

16. Solanus Casey, Letter to Margaret LeDoux, April 30, 1945, "Collected Writings," Vol. I, p. 143.
17. Ibid.
18. Ibid., p. 144.
19. Ibid., p. 143.
20. Michael H. Crosby, O.F.M. Cap., *Thank God Ahead of Time* (Chicago: Franciscan Herald Press, 1985), pp. 9-10.
21. Mead et al., op. cit., p. 45.

Chapter 2

1. Crosby, op. cit., p. 12.
2. Ibid., p. 13.
3. Derum, op. cit., p. 26.
4. Mead et al., op. cit., p. 91.
5. Derum, op. cit., p. 34.
6. Ibid., pp. 38-39.
7. Crosby, op. cit., p. 13.
8. Ibid., p. 228.
9. Derum, op. cit., p. 41.
10. Ibid., p. 26.
11. Mead et al., op. cit., p. 42.
12. Albert Britt, *An America That Was* (Barre, Mass.: Barre Publishers, 1964), p. 31.
13. Derum, op. cit., pp. 39-40.
14. Crosby, op. cit., pp. 13-14.
15. Derum, op. cit., p. 42.
16. Mead et al., op. cit., p. 6.
17. Derum, op. cit., p. 44.
18. Ibid., p. 46.
19. Crosby, op. cit., p. 16.
20. Ibid., pp. 15-16.
21. Derum, op. cit., pp. 46-47.
22. Ibid., pp. 48-49.
23. Ibid.
24. Ibid.

Chapter 3

1. Derum, op. cit., p. 51.
2. Ibid., p. 53.
3. McDonald, op. cit., p. 206.
4. Ibid., p. 207.
5. Sowell, op. cit., p. 40, as taken from Andrew Greeley, *That Most Distressful Nation* (p. 93), and Carl Wittke, *The Irish in America* (p. 91).
6. McDonald, op. cit., pp. 208-209.
7. Derum, op. cit., p. 56.
8. Ibid., p. 57.
9. McDonald, op. cit., p. 207, as taken from *Catholic Citizen*, June 26, 1896.
10. Derum, op. cit., p. 57.
11. Ibid., p. 58.
12. Solanus Casey, Letter to Father Bonaventure Frey, Aug. 23, 1896, "Collected Writings," Vol. I, p. 19.
13. Catherine Bicknell, *St. Bonaventure Monastery: 1883-1983* (Detroit: Fidelity, 1983), pp. 20-22.
14. Solanus Casey, Jan. 13, 1897, Vice-Postulator's Archives, Detroit.
15. Donald Attwater, *The Penguin Dictionary of Saints* (Middlesex, England: Penguin Books, 1965), pp. 140-141.
16. Bicknell, op. cit., p. 42.
17. Derum, op. cit., p. 73.
18. Bicknell, op. cit., p. 43.
19. Solanus Casey, "Collected Writings."
20. Solanus Casey, "Attestation," July 20, 1898, Vice-Postulator's Archives, Detroit.

Chapter 4

1. Derum, op. cit., pp. 77-78.
2. Crosby, op. cit., pp. 39-40.
3. Solanus Casey, "Statement," July 5, 1901, Vice-Postulator's Archives, Detroit.

4. Father Boniface Goldhausen, "Collected Writings," Vol. I, p. 12.
5. Solanus Casey, "Notebook 9," June 13, 1902, "Collected Writings," Vol. I, p. 15.
6. Derum, op. cit., p. 82.
7. Ibid.
8. Solanus Casey, Letter to Ella Traynor, Feb. 21, 1904, "Collected Writings," Vol. I, p. 71.
9. Crosby, op. cit., p. 44.
10. Derum, op. cit., p. 85.
11. Solanus Casey, Letter to James Casey, Jan. 29, 1943, "Collected Writings," Vol. I, p. 228.

Chapter 5

1. Jerry E. Patterson, *The City of New York* (New York: Harry N. Abrams, Inc., 1978), p. 198.
2. Stephen Longstreet, *City on Two Rivers* (New York: Hawthorn Books, Inc., 1975), pp. 114-116.
3. Bicknell, op. cit., p. 23.
4. Crosby, op. cit., p. 48.
5. "The Brother Sacristan," poem by Msgr. Edward Casey.
6. Derum, op. cit., p. 89.
7. Crosby, op. cit., p. 59.
8. Solanus Casey, Letter to James Casey, Jan. 29, 1943, "Collected Writings," Vol. I, p. 234.
9. Crosby, op. cit., p. 51.
10. Ibid.
11. Solanus Casey, "Notebook 9," c. 1909, "Collected Writings," Vol. I, p. 18.
12. Sr. Agrippina Petrosino, Interview with Michael H. Crosby, O.F.M. Cap.
13. Crosby, op. cit., pp. 54-55.
14. Petrosino, Interview with Crosby.
15. Crosby, op. cit., pp. 53-54.
16. Ibid., p. 279.
17. Ibid., p. 64.

18. Brother Leo Wollenweber, Interview with Catherine Odell, June 12, 1986.
19. Solanus Casey, "Notebook 9," Nov. 25, 1910, "Collected Writings," Vol. I, p. 19.
20. Derum, op. cit., p. 91.
21. Solanus Casey, Letter to James Casey, Jan. 29, 1943, "Collected Writings," Vol. I, p. 230.
22. Derum, op. cit., p. 92.
23. Ibid., p. 95.
24. Wollenweber, Interview with Odell.
25. Patterson, op. cit., p. 215.
26. Solanus Casey, Letter to Margaret LeDoux, Jan. 3 and 5, 1916, "Collected Writings," Vol. I, pp. 5-6.
27. Derum, op. cit., p. 100.
28. Solanus Casey, "Notebook 9," June 16, 1918, "Collected Writings," Vol. I, p. 19.
29. Solanus Casey, Letter to Margaret LeDoux, July 16, 1918, "Collected Writings," Vol. IA (Appendix to Vol. I), p. 7.
30. Crosby, op. cit., p. 274.

Chapter 6

1. Wollenweber, op. cit., p. 6.
2. Crosby, op. cit., pp. 75-77.
3. Solanus Casey, Letter to Margaret LeDoux, July 24, 1921, "Collected Writings," Vol. IA, p. 9.
4. Wollenweber, op. cit., p. 6.
5. Derum, op. cit., p. 101.
6. Crosby, op. cit., p. 81.
7. Our Lady of the Angels Friary Chronicle (Harlem, N.Y.), Jan. 14, 1922.
8. Solanus Casey, "Catholic News," "Collected Writings," Vol. I, p. 74.
9. Crosby, op. cit., p. 82.
10. Derum, op. cit., p. 103.
11. Solanus Casey, "Notebook 1," "Collected Works."
12. Ibid.

13. Ibid.
14. Solanus Casey, Letter to Father Benno Aichinger, Jan. 25, 1924, "Collected Writings," Vol. I, p. 83.
15. Derum, op. cit., pp. 105-107.
16. Ibid., p. 105.
17. Wollenweber, op. cit., p. 7.
18. Solanus Casey, Letter to James Casey, July 18, 1938, "Collected Writings," Vol. I, p. 198.

Chapter 7

1. Bicknell, op. cit., p. 39.
2. Ibid., p. 27.
3. Father Marion Roessler, "Written Reports," p. 4.
4. Solanus Casey, Letter to Margaret LeDoux, July 16, 1937, "Collected Writings," Vol. I, p. 18.
5. Solanus Casey, Letter to Sister Cecilia Eagen, Nov. 7, 1947, "Collected Writings," Vol. II, p. 175.
6. Derum, op. cit., p. 11.
7. Solanus Casey, Letter to Margaret LeDoux, Oct. 19, 1954, "Collected Writings," Vol. IA, p. 35.
8. Father Cosmas Niedhammer, Aug. 16, 1975, "Written Reports," p. 5.
9. Father Herman Buss, Nov. 10, 1969, "Written Reports," p. 3.
10. Niedhammer, op. cit., p. 3.
11. Derum, op. cit., p. 112.
12. Crosby, op. cit., p. 117.
13. Buss, op. cit., p. 3.
14. Ibid., p. 5.
15. Charles K. Hyde, *Detroit: An Industrial History Guide* (Detroit: S.I.A., 1982), p. 23.
16. Crosby, op. cit., p. 114.
17. Thomas R. Frazier, ed., *The Private Side of American History*, Vol. II, article by Edward Robb Ellis entitled "What the Depression Did to People," p. 199.
18. Hyde, op. cit., p. 23.

19. Crosby, op. cit., p. 117.
20. Catherine Bicknell, *Breaking Bread and Mending Spirits* (Detroit: Fidelity, 1979), p. 16.
21. Ibid., p. 17.
22. Frazier, op. cit., article by Ellis, p. 200.
23. Ibid., p. 214.
24. Bicknell, *Breaking Bread*, op. cit., p. 18.
25. Buss, op. cit., p. 6.
26. Charles A. and Mary R. Beard, *A Basic History of the United States* (Philadelphia: The Blakiston Co., 1944), p. 452.
27. Martha A. Houlihan, June 21, 1977, "Written Reports," p. 1.
28. William Tremblay, Dec. 12, 1962, "Written Reports," p. 54.
29. Excerpts from St. Bonaventure Friary Chronicle (Detroit, Mich.), p. 4.
30. Mrs. Mary Therese McHugh, Dec. 15, 1978, "Written Reports."
31. Tremblay, op. cit., p. 56.

Chapter 8

1. St. Bonaventure Friary Chronicle, p. 5.
2. Father Lawrence Merton, "Written Reports," p. 35.
3. Father Marion Roessler, "Written Reports," p. 48.
4. Derum, op. cit., p. 170.
5. Crosby, op. cit., p. 128.
6. Derum, op. cit., pp. 168-169.
7. Tremblay, op. cit., p. 59.
8. Mrs. Agnes Juergens, Oct. 27, 1978, "Written Reports."
9. Derum, op. cit., p. 165.
10. Crosby, op. cit., p. 130.
11. Derum, op. cit., p. 189.
12. Solanus Casey, Letter to James Casey, Jan. 29, 1943, "Collected Writings," Vol. I, p. 217.
13. Crosby, op. cit., pp. 132-133.
14. Solanus Casey, Letter to Father Maurice Casey, Dec. 15, 1938, "Collected Writings," Vol. I, pp. 147-148.

15. Father Michael Cefai, Jan. 10, 1968, "Written Reports."
16. Solanus Casey, Letter to Margaret LeDoux, Jan. 26, 1937, "Collected Writings," Vol. IA, p. 16.
17. Hyde, op. cit., p. 123.
18. Derum, op. cit., pp. 192-193.
19. Crosby, op. cit., p. 135.
20. Mrs. Leona Gergely, March 29, 1978, "Written Reports," p. 77.
21. Wollenweber, Interview with Odell.
22. Derum, op. cit., pp. 195-196.
23. Ibid., pp. 153-154.
24. Brother Daniel Brady, Letter to Father Michael H. Crosby, Feb. 20, 1983.
25. St. Bonaventure Friary Chronicle, p. 10.
26. Solanus Casey, Letter to Margaret LeDoux, Nov. 17, 1942, "Collected Writings," Vol. IA, p. 21.
27. Ibid., p. 23.
28. Crosby, op. cit., pp. 147-148.

Chapter 9

1. *The Annals of America* (Chicago: Encyclopaedia Britannica, 1968), p. xli.
2. Solanus Casey, Letter to Muriel Krausman, June 9, 1946, "Collected Writings," Vol. II, p. 97.
3. Crosby, op. cit., p. 149.
4. Solanus Casey, Letter to Father Marion Roessler, July 9, 1945, "Collected Writings," Vol. II, p. 144.
5. Crosby, op. cit., p. 151.
6. Ibid., pp. 148-149.
7. Wollenweber, op. cit., p. 8.
8. Niedhammer, op. cit., p. 45.
9. Crosby, op. cit., p. 157.
10. Solanus Casey, Letter to Margaret LeDoux, Sept. 9, 1945, "Collected Writings," Vol. IIA (Appendix to Vol. II), p. 24.
11. Solanus Casey, Letter to Ray Garland, Oct. 22, 1945, "Collected Writings," Vol. II, p. 149.

12. Father Walter O'Brien, Interview with Father Michael H. Crosby, Jan. 11, 1983.
13. Solanus Casey, "Always Christmas Eve," his poem in "Collected Writings," Vol. II, p. 156.
14. Solanus Casey, Letter to Monsignor Edward Casey, March 28, 1946, "Collected Writings," Vol. I, p. 176.
15. Father Barnabas Keck, Interview with Father Michael H. Crosby, Jan. 11, 1983.

Chapter 10

1. Excerpts from St. Felix Friary Chronicle (Huntington, Ind.), Vol. I, p. 1.
2. Ibid.
3. Solanus Casey, Letter to Belle Lyke, May 22, 1946, "Collected Writings," Vol. II, p. 175.
4. Ibid..
5. Derum, op. cit., p. 239.
6. Ibid., p. 236.
7. Ibid., pp. 236-237.
8. Father Ambrose De Groot, Aug. 17, 1977, "Written Reports," p. 15.
9. Ibid., p. 14.
10. St. Felix Friary Chronicle, Vol. I, p. 2.
11. Ibid., pp. 4-5.
12. Solanus Casey, Letter to Mrs. Leon Herkenrath, Jan. 22, 1948, "Collected Writings," Vol. I, p. 241.
13. Father Blase Gitzen, Taped interview with Father Michael H. Crosby.
14. Crosby, op. cit., p. 209.
15. Father Blase Gitzen, Nov. 14, 1969, "Written Reports."
16. St. Felix Friary Chronicle, Vol. I, p. 6.
17. Derum, op. cit., pp. 234-235.
18. Crosby, op. cit., p. 195.
19. De Groot, op. cit., p. 16.
20. Crosby, op. cit., p. 201.

21. Victory Noll Sisters, Interview with Catherine Anthony (Odell), April, 1977.
22. Monsignor James P. Conroy, Interview with Catherine Odell, 1982.
23. Victory Noll Sisters, Interview with Odell.
24. Father Francis (Thomas Aquinas) Heidenreich, Interview with Catherine Anthony (Odell), April, 1977.
25. Solanus Casey, Letter to Mr. and Mrs. Frank LeDoux, May 17, 1950, "Collected Writings," Vol. II, p. 31.
26. Crosby, op. cit., as taken from Benedict Groeschel, *Spiritual Passages: The Psychology of Spiritual Development* (New York: Crossroad Publishing Co., 1983), pp. 184-185.
27. Cefai, op. cit.
28. St. Felix Friary Chronicle, Vol. II, p. 6.
29. Mercedes Uhfeil, March 13, 1977, "Written Reports," p. 85.
30. Brother Booker Ashe, July 14, 1975, "Written Reports," p. 2.
31. Ibid., p. 3.
32. Mrs. Rita Evison, "Written Reports," pp. 82-83.
33. St. Felix Friary Chronicle, Vol. II, p. 10.
34. Frank J. Brady, May 28, 1978, "Written Reports," p. 5.
35. St. Felix Friary Chronicle, Vol. II, p. 12.

Chapter 11

1. St. Felix Friary Chronicle, Vol. II, p. 12.
2. Ibid.
3. Crosby, op. cit., p. 226.
4. Ibid., p. 226.
5. Bicknell, *St. Bonaventure Monastery: 1883-1983*, op. cit., p. 43.
6. Father Dan Crosby, June 7, 1984, "Written Reports."
7. Merton, op. cit.
8. Ibid.
9. Brother Ignatius Milne, Interview with Catherine Odell, 1982.

10. Wollenweber, Interview with Odell.
11. St. Bonaventure Chronicle, p. 12.
12. Jerry Sullivan, "Life in the Monastery in the Heart of Detroit," in the *Detroit News*, Dec. 2, 1956.
13. St. Bonaventure Friary Chronicle, p. 12.
14. Derum, op. cit., pp. 257-258.
15. Ibid., p. 258.
16. Father Michael Dalton, Nov. 20, 1977, "Written Reports."
17. Crosby, op. cit., p. 241.
18. Ibid., p. 242.
19. Ibid., p. 241.
20. Derum, op. cit., p. 266.
21. Father Gerald Walker, "Written Reports," p. 68.
22. Crosby, op. cit., p. 242.
23. Walker, op. cit., p. 69.
24. Derum, op. cit., p. 275.
25. Crosby, op. cit., p. 244.
26. St. Felix Friary Chronicle, Vol. II, p. 13.

Chapter 12

1. Derum, op. cit., pp. 20-22.
2. De Groot, op. cit., p. 17.
3. *Detroit News*, Aug. 4, 1957.
4. Wollenweber, Interview with Odell.
5. Mary Casey Molloy, March 20, 1977, "Written Reports," pp. 37-38.

BIBLIOGRAPHY

The Annals of America, Vol. 16. Chicago: Encyclopaedia Britannica, 1968.

Attwater, Donald. *The Penguin Dictionary of Saints*. Middlesex, England: Penguin, 1965.

Bicknell, Catherine. *Breaking Bread and Mending Spirits*. Detroit: Fidelity, 1979.

_____. *St. Bonaventure Monastery, 1883-1983*. Detroit: Fidelity, 1983.

Beard, Charles A., and Mary R. *A Basic History of the United States*. Philadelphia: The Blakiston Co., 1944.

Britt, Albert. *An America That Was*. Barre, Mass.: Barre, 1964.

Capuchin Century Book. Detroit: Capuchin Friars, 1957.

Crosby, Michael H., O.F.M. Cap. *Thank God Ahead of Time: The Life and Spirituality of Solanus Casey*. Chicago: Franciscan Herald Press, 1985.

Derum, James Patrick. *The Porter of Saint Bonaventure* Detroit: Fidelity, 1968.

Dolan, Jay P. *The American Catholic Experience*. Garden City, N.Y.: Doubleday, 1985.

Hyde, Charles K. *Detroit: An Industrial History Guide*. Detroit: S.I.A., 1982.

Longstreet, Stephen. *City on Two Rivers*. New York: Hawthorn Books, 1975.

McDonald, Sister M. Justille, M.A. *History of the Irish in Wisconsin in the Nineteenth Century*. Washington, D.C.: The Catholic University of America Press, 1954.

Mead, Howard, Jill Dean, and Susan Smith. *Portrait of the Past: A Photographic Journey Through Wisconsin*. Madison, Wis.: Wisconsin Tales and Trails, 1971.

O'Grady, Joseph P. *How the Irish Became Americans.* Boston: Twayne Publishers, Div. of G.K. Hall & Co., 1973.

Patterson, Jerry E. *The City of New York.* New York: Harry N. Abrams, 1978.

The Private Side of American History, Vol. II, edited by Thomas R. Frazier. New York: Harcourt Brace Jovanovich, 1975.

Sowell, Thomas. *Ethnic America.* New York: Basic Books, 1981.